GERMAN MOUNTAIN TROOPS
1942–45

CASEMATE | ILLUSTRATED

CASEMATE | ILLUSTRATED

GERMAN MOUNTAIN TROOPS 1942–45

YVES BÉRAUD

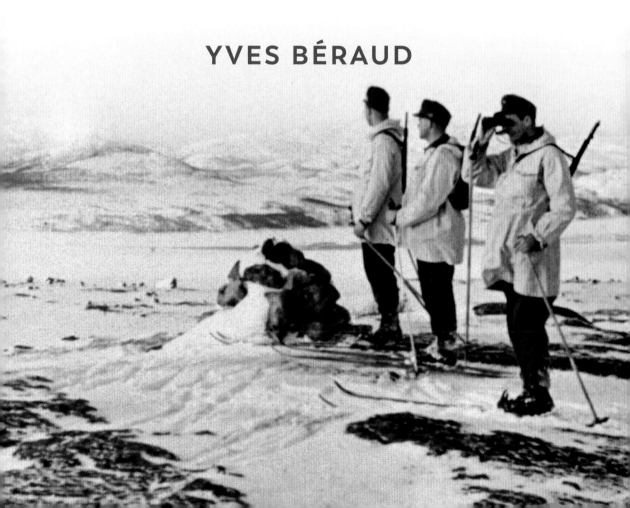

CASEMATE | ILLUSTRATED

CIS0022

This book is published in cooperation with and under license from Memorabilia Editions. Adapted from *Gebirgstruppen: Les troupes de montagne allemandes 1935–1945 en couleurs* by Memorabilia Editions, 2017.

Print Edition: ISBN 978-1-61200-9469
Digital Edition: ISBN 978-1-61200-9476

Design by Battlefield Design
Translated by Alan McKay
Printed and bound in the Czech Republic by FINIDR, s.r.o.

CASEMATE PUBLISHERS (US)
Telephone (610) 853-9131
Fax (610) 853-9146
Email: casemate@casematepublishers.com
www.casematepublishers.com

CASEMATE PUBLISHERS (UK)
Telephone (01865) 241249
Email: casemate-uk@casematepublishers.co.uk
www.casematepublishers.co.uk

Title page: *Jäger* carried out patrols in the vast spaces between the fortified positions, on skis or on foot, enabling them to extend their knowledge of the terrain and to prepare for their baptism of fire. Light was weak during the winter months, which did little to assist with observation. (Ehrt Archives)

Contents page map: Operation *Bagration*. (Original US Govt document, uploaded by General Patton/ www.jewishvirtuallibrary.org/jsource/ww2/easterneurope8.html)

Contents page image: Only limited winter operations were carried out on the German side. Here *Gebirgsjäger* are heading to their departure line in the Sinyavino region, supported by Sturmgeschützen. These machines were fitted with wider tracks (*Ostketten*), with the *Jäger* moving along the road in columns, and as tirailleurs over open ground. (DR, War News Chronicles)

Note: Due to constraints of space, the appendices only appear in *German Mountain Troops 1939-42*. These are Appendix 1: Organization Chart; Appendix 2: Tactical Symbols; Appendix 3: Abbreviations

The author thanks Bundesarchiv Koblenz, CIRIP, ECPAD, Cahiers des Troupes de Montagne, Anciens du Maquis de l'Oisans, Ufficio Storico Esercito, Istituto Resistenza Cuneo, Gli Ultimi, Musée des Chasseurs–Vincennes, Anciens du Bataillon Berthier, Le Haut Pays, US Army, US DoD, UNADIF, Musée de la Résistance Azuréenne, Musée des Troupes de Montagne; as well as Messrs. Allain, André, Angelini, Arena, Barbi, Barkats, Bellec, Henri and N. Béraud, Casarotto, Chanel, Chassé, Contino, Davrainville, Della Siega, Demouzon, Dory, O. Duhot, Dupré, S. Ehrt, R.Eiermann, Fortier, Frondeville, Frossard, de Galbert, Gallion, Gatinel, Alain Gesgon—CIRIP, Hartmann, Hascher, Haupt, Hecht, Lagier-Brun, Le Faou, Lenz, Lissner, Lombard, Maire, Masse, Maignon, Morand, Münch, Neuner, Niklaus, Noblet, Novak, Passemard, Pecile, Pénidon, Pisano, Turinetti di Priero, Pröhl, Prudent, Rietzler, Rogger, Sabon, Sandri, Schroeder, Schubert, Simonin, Speer, Stöhr, Tabouis, Thiry, Urschiz, Vasserot, Verdenal, and Vollaire.

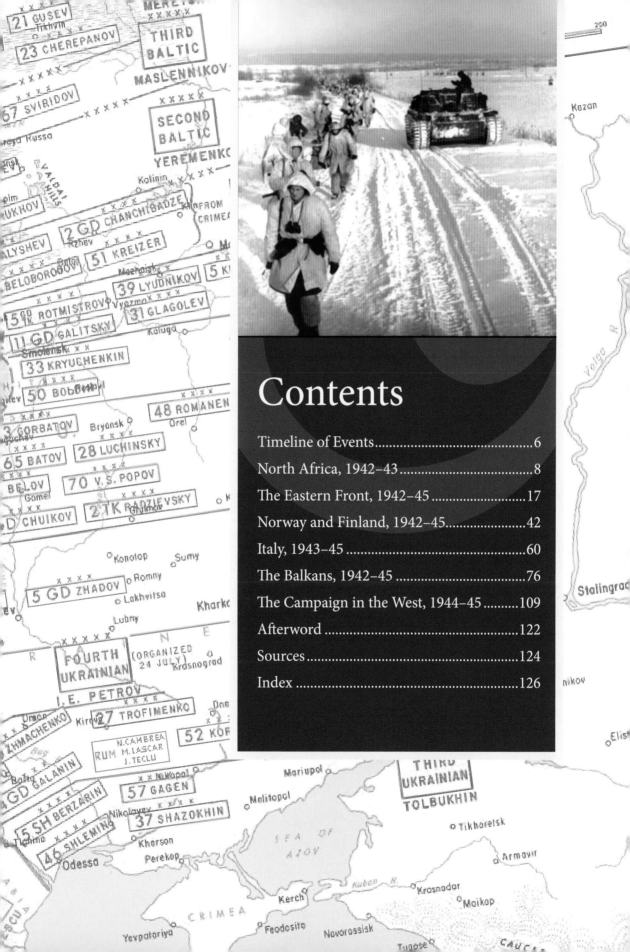

Contents

Timeline of Events 6

North Africa, 1942–43 8

The Eastern Front, 1942–45 17

Norway and Finland, 1942–45 42

Italy, 1943–45 60

The Balkans, 1942–45 76

The Campaign in the West, 1944–45 109

Afterword 122

Sources 124

Index 126

| Timeline of Events

In 1942, the *Gebirgsjäger* were scattered across Europe and North Africa, from the frozen wastes of Cape North at the northern tip of Norway, to the blistering desert heat of North Africa with Rommel's Panzerarmee Afrika, which would soon be locked in combat with the British Eight Army at El Alamein, a pivotal moment in the war. In Eastern Europe, across to the Caucasus Mountains, the attritional battle at Stalingrad would witness the German 6th Army being devoured by the Red Army, the defining event of the war that would see the Wehrmacht, including several mountain corps, shrink inexorably toward Central Europe and the borders of the Reich. 1944/5 saw many of the mountain divisions deployed piecemeal, often in their famous *Feuerwehr*—fire brigade—role, to combat insurgencies in the Balkans, in Italy, and in the South of France, campaigns characterized by brutal atrocities.

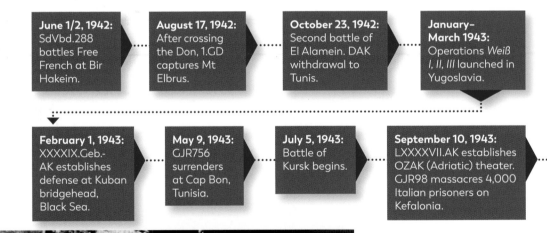

June 1/2, 1942:
SdVbd.288 battles Free French at Bir Hakeim.

August 17, 1942:
After crossing the Don, 1.GD captures Mt Elbrus.

October 23, 1942:
Second battle of El Alamein. DAK withdrawal to Tunis.

January– March 1943:
Operations *Weiß I, II, III* launched in Yugoslavia.

February 1, 1943:
XXXXIX.Geb.-AK establishes defense at Kuban bridgehead, Black Sea.

May 9, 1943:
GJR756 surrenders at Cap Bon, Tunisia.

July 5, 1943:
Battle of Kursk begins.

September 10, 1943:
LXXXXVII.AK establishes OZAK (Adriatic) theater. GJR98 massacres 4,000 Italian prisoners on Kefalonia.

Gebirgsjäger, Panzerfäuste at the ready, wait in the vicinity of Monte Cassino for the Allied tanks. (DR)

A heavy machine-gun crew awaiting the next Soviet attack in the Volkhov sector. The tension on their faces is clear. (Colored photo "By Lex," DR)

January–May 1944: 5.GD in combat at Monte Cassino.

June 23, 1944: Soviet summer offensive, Operation *Bagration*, opens. Dietl killed in plane crash.

August 1, 1944: The Warsaw Uprising begins.

August 15, 1944: Allied landing in Provence.

August 25, 1944: Kesselring establishes Gothic Line in Apennines.

September 15, 1944: Finland informally declares war on Germany.

January 1–25, 1945: Operation *Nordwind* in Alsace-Lorraine/Rhineland.

January 22, 1945: XXXXVIII.AK clashes with Red Army at frozen Oder River.

February 1945: V.SS-Gebirgs-Armee-Korps withdraws from Balkans.

May 8, 1945: XXXXIX. Geb.-AK surrenders in Bohemia-Moravia.

May 14/15, 1945: Tito's partisans victorious at battle of Poljana.

| North Africa, 1942–43

Following the proclamation of the Berlin–Rome Axis of November 1, 1936, the Italo-German Pact of Steel of May 22, 1939, and, lastly, on September 27, 1940, the Tripartite Pact between Germany, Italy, and Japan, Adolf Hitler issued his directive *Führerweisung* Nr. 32, dated June 11, 1941, as a post-*Barbarossa* strategy. The ambitious plan was to link up with Japanese forces advancing west across Asia, with a northern German pincer sweeping south through the Caucasus, and a southern German–Italian pincer pushing east across Suez to occupy the Middle Eastern oilfields.

2.(Gebirgs)Kompanie/Sonderverband 288

In Libya *Führerweisung* Nr. 32 was entrusted to Sonderverband 288 (whose 2.(Gebirgs) Kompanie is of particular interest), in spite of the fact that no mountain units were thought to be needed in North Africa: the Djebel, the range of hills that stretches from Morocco— where the German–Italian Armistice Commission was in place—to Egypt, is not high and fighting took place for the most part along this coastal strip. Sonderverband 288 was one of the two major components of the Orientkorps, the major command given the task of realizing this "grand vision." Stationed in Greece, it was placed under command of *General der Luftwaffe* Erwin Felmy, who, as pilot 2nd lieutenant, had seen action with the German

Expeditionary Corps in Palestine during World War I. Leaving Greece, this "special" unit was originally supposed to deploy to Syria, backed by Vichy troops, but the British and the Free French decided otherwise. The minimum objective—to disrupt Allied oil supplies—was high on the Axis agenda.

At Potsdam (Hohenlohe Kaserne), on July 24, 1941, a variety of units had been brought together, enabling a so-called "special" unit, Sonderverband 288, to be formed. ("Special" was defined by the way the unit was organized and the missions with which it was to be entrusted.)

Under command of Colonel Otto Menton—Menton had been a close friend of

A deep-penetration patrol returns, on the southern flank of the Afrikakorps. (DR)

This M40 helmet, initially painted in Panzer gray, has had a coat of sand-colored paint applied with a spray-gun. The escutcheon with the national eagle can still be seen quite clearly. (Private collection)

Issued to the earlier contingents of mountain troops, this standard *Mantel* (greatcoat) has been tailored in khaki cloth. It bears the edelweiss sewn on the sleeve and the *Schulterklappen* (shoulder flaps) of an *Unterfeldwebel*, a staff sergeant.

General Erwin Rommel since the Great War—the unit comprised a *Stab*, and a *Stabskp* that included an armored reconnaissance platoon (*Pz.Spähtrupp*), a reconnaissance platoon (*Aufklärungszug*), and a printing section (*Druckereitrupp*) for tracts printed in Arabic, as well as 2.Gebirgsjäger-Kp, whose skills might prove useful in the mountainous areas of the Near East, beyond the Nile. Included too were 3.Schützen-Kp, a fusilier company; 4.MG.Kp; 5.Pz. Jg.-Kp., including a platoon of Sturmgeschütze IIIs; 7.Pionier-Kp; and a Nachtrichten-Kp (signal company). Also there to add strength was 1.Sonder-Kp, from the Lehr-Rgt.z.b.V.800 of the Abwehr—the future Brandenburg Regiment—made up mainly of Germans with experience of the Near and Middle East, and former French legionnaires. This unit is out of the scope of this study since it only arrived at the beginning of 1942, and being out in front of the Afrikakorps (Deutsches Afrikakorps, or DAK), carried out operations that had nothing to do with those of the SdVbd (Sonderverband), such as preparing to capture the crossing points on the Suez Canal, or a raid as far south as Lake Chad.

In all, SdVbd.288 had a total strength of 2,000 men, and comprised some 12 subunits, including a medical company with 12 tropical disease specialists, native auxiliary troops and interpreters (Arabic in particular), and even an oil and water research group. Each subunit was from a particular arm (or specialty) and its personnel bore the appropriate colors on shoulder flaps and cap piping. Each subunit was able to carry out specific missions in its area of expertise and independently, but it could also take part in so-called "special" missions requiring several fields of expertise.

From October 1–24, 1941, SdVbd.288 was sent to Greece to perfect its training. With the Orientkorps command post already there, at Lavrion, the Stab/SdVbd.288 set itself up at Cape Sounion. In mid-November, the first elements were dispatched by plane via Crete to Libya where the British Eighth Army was trying to regain the initiative through Operation *Crusader*, launched on November 17 and known as Operation *Winterschlacht* (*Winter*

Soldaten-Kino.

Das Kino-Großprogramm im bombensicheren Soldaten-Kino lockt unsere Sonntagsurlauber. Also hinein!

Opportunities for relaxation were few and far between on the North African front. These *Gebirgsjäger* from 2.(Geb.)/SdVbd.288 take advantage of the new Derna cinema. The caption of this propaganda photograph suggests it was bombproof.

Operation) by the Germans in the Afrikakorps. Two platoons, I. and III., from 2.(Geb.)/SdVbd.288 under *Oberleutnant* (First Lieutenant) Thumser were rushed to Benghazi, Libya, to take part in the highly urgent (with no interpreters, to be used as "simple" infantry) making up of Sperrverband Daumiller—the "Daumiller mobile barrage detachment"—named after the *Hauptmann* (captain) in command, or alternatively, Sperrverband Poseïdon. This element was engaged at once under command of the 90. leichte Division[1] which had been entrusted with the defense of the Benghazi–Adjedabia sector since mid-December, and which remained the administrative support unit of the SdVbd.288 for the rest of the campaign.

A threat had been identified which needed a "special" reaction: the raids carried out by the British Long Range Desert Group (LRDG), especially along the coast, by E Force under Major General D. W. Reid, against airfields, logistics facilities and other targets in western Cyrenaica. On January 13, Second Lieutenant Werner Kost, a platoon leader in 2.(Geb)/288, reconnoitering out on one of the rocky outcrops near Marada oasis, a good place for long-distance observation, wounded and captured an LRDG officer, Captain Simms. It became clear that a large British offensive was in the offing.

At Syrte, the 90. leichte Division had to ensure the defense of the Marada–Marsa el Brega position until the beginning of February. In response to a massive infantry attack, two Panzer counterattacks were carried out from this line on December 28/29, inflicting heavy losses on the British 22nd Tank Brigade but enemy pressure was so great that on the 31st, the 90th fell back onto a better fortified line. New Year's Day was marked by both sides firing off tracer projectiles.

This German withdrawal proved inadequate and in spite of *Crusader* ending on January 15, the Germans had to abandon Halfaya Pass, "the fires of hell" pass, on January 17, where they had resisted for weeks in blocking the enemy. In early February, Sperrverband Daumiller was deployed to take up positions at Marada oasis to form a static blocking position, a *Sperriegel*, and at the same time protect the DAK's flanks. It was joined by other German

---

1 What was left of the administrative support unit of SdVbd.288 for the remainder of the campaign.

The cloth and cork topee issued in Germany, worn here by Second Lieutenant W. Kost, was quickly abandoned.

The Sonderverband 288 escutcheon, as used by the whole Orientkorps, showing a rising sun surrounded by palm trees (*Sonne und Palmen*). The woven or embroidered BEVo (Bernd Ewald Vorsteher) model for officers was sewn on the sleeve. The copper alloy version (Kost Archives) was worn by 2.(Geb.)Kp, and sold in the *Soldatenheim*, the soldiers' mess, before they left for the African theater.

Lieutenant Kost models the typical uniform worn by 2.(Geb.) / Sonderverband 288: tropical Heer field jacket, pilot's yellow scarf, loose Luftwaffe trousers, and *Bergschuhe* (mountain boots). (Werner Kost Archive)

and Italian elements which were to prove indispensable if they were to hold this key point before the big offensive the Panzerarmee Afrika launched on the 23rd toward Msus, which was taken on the 27th. This forced the British to fall back towards El Mecheli, taken a few days later by Kampfgruppe Marcks, which then rushed towards Ridotta Rhegina.

Beyond that, the desert stretched out without any landmarks. The Sperrverband carried out patrols by plotting mileage and using compasses, just like the LRDG. Most of their vehicles were captured from the British; the unit was afforded a Fieseler Storch for reconnaissance missions. At the end of January 1942, Captain Borchardt replaced Daumiller, who was sent back to Cape Sounion.

The remainder of SdVbd.288, in particular its heavy weapons, joined the rest of the unit in North Africa in January/February 1942 with Colonel Menton. Those remaining at Cape Sounion made up a dedicated training unit. Early fighting in the desert showed that earlier plans of using them operationally as mentioned above were impossible to put into practice. Three *Kampfgruppen* were therefore made up and it was in this more flexible configuration that SdVbd.288 was engaged, still within the 90. leichte Division, after March 10. The hope within the Panzerarmee Afrika was that it would have a unit capable of opening a path to the Suez Canal and the Nile, and then to the oilfields of the Arabian Peninsula.

On May 26, the Panzerarmee Afrika's big offensive opened, aiming to take Tobruk. The 90's mission was to outflank Eighth Army positions by the south and to take El Adem in order to prevent a withdrawal from Tobruk and cut the British off from their logistic support base situated between Trigh Capuzzo and the sea. The British strongpoints were bypassed one by one, the priority being speed. The *Gebirgsjäger*, fresh from renewed training, were able to advance over open terrain, across minefields, and even engaged in some hand-to-hand fighting. They were involved in taking the fortified site at Got el Ualeb then that at Knightsbridge, after crossing a minefield breach made by Italian sappers from the 101st Motorized Division Trieste, with the *Jäger* riding on vehicle fenders under enemy fire, in a sandstorm

During the night of June 1/2, 1942, SdVbd.288, reinforcing the Italian Ariete Division and within a *Kampfgruppe* commanded by the Panzerarmee Afrika's *Pionier-Führer*, Colonel Hecker, took part in the fighting to break Allied resistance at Bir Hakeim.

The *Tropenmütze* had the arm's *Jägergrün* (rifle green)-colored piping, above the national roundel and officer's silver braiding on the top. The arm's piping was dispensed with in July 1942. (Private collection)

The Afrikakorps cuff band, woven by BEVo, was sewn 15 centimeters above the bottom of the right-hand sleeve. From July 18, 1941 onward, it could be worn by personnel who had spent at least two months in this theater of operations.

The commemorative campaign cuff band "*Afrika*" came into being from January 15, 1943, replacing the "*Afrikakorps*" band, in theory at least. This distinction applied to soldiers who had spent at least six months in the North African theater of operations (reduced to four in July 1943) or having been wounded or awarded a medal (Iron Cross or German Cross in Gold), or posthumously. It was made of camel hair (*Kamelhaarstoff*). The model shown here bears a reception number on the reverse side, an "RBNr." (Private collection)

Bir Hakeim was held by 4,400 *Français Libres* (Free French), under General Marie-Pierre Koenig, forcing the Germans onto a wide southern detour. The Germans were unable to prevent the French from withdrawing from their position once the precious extra time the British command had wanted had been gained beyond all expectation. In spite of heavy losses—all their officers were killed or wounded—the French finally abandoned their positions during the night of June 9/10.

On June 24, the Panzerarmee Afrika crossed the border into Egypt. On the 30th, it reached Mersa Matruh, exhausted, with only 70 panzers operational. Then, on July 12, it reached the mouth of the El Alamein corridor, a narrow coastal strip, and farther south, the north–south-oriented Ruweisat Hills, the Qattara Depression and the quick sands of the Great Sand Sea (some 72,000 square kilometers), that was inaccessible to armor.

During July and August, the first battle of El Alamein took place, attacks and counterattacks conducted over a relatively small sector of ground where Rommel was forced to engage, ending his hopes of resuming the war of movement at which he excelled. As his overstretched supply lines proved increasingly problematic, his best hope was to prevent his adversary from recovering and reconstituting his forces, and capturing his depots. 2./SdVbd.288 suffered heavy losses: at the end of the fighting, only 38 men were still operational, with all the officers unfit for service.

August 30 marked the end of this first battle: the British had stopped the Germans on the crests of Alam el Halfa and Hill 102. Fearing another British counterattack, Rommel went onto the defensive and established almost impregnable positions: the terrain that had helped the Allies during the first battle of El Alamein, was now going to help the Germans.

In Tunisia, in the Dra-el-Mamir sector, GJR756 fought in support of Tiger 1 tanks. (GJR 756 Association)

After six weeks rebuilding its forces, the Eighth Army, with its new C-in-C, General Bernard Montgomery, had established a ratio of 2 to 1 in men and armor and was able to go over into the attack on October 23, 1942 in the decisive second battle of El Alamein.

By the end of October, SdVbd.288 was in reserve, building up its coastal defense strength in the Mersa Matruh sector. It was therefore given the difficult mission of covering the Panzerarmee Afrika's withdrawal to Tunisia. It became Panzergrenadier-Regiment Afrika on October 31, 1942, while still continuing to bear its original designation, according to the documents.

On November 1, the unit fell back through the Halfaya Pass jammed with vehicles and pounded by British bombers. Rommel wanted to reduce the front he had to defend, on favorable ground, in order to face the American forces that had landed in Algeria and Morocco during Operation *Torch* in November 1942, all the while facing the British since his defeat at El Alamein over a rapid and continuous withdrawal. He was obliged to fall back on Tunisia.

On January 23, Tripoli fell to the Eighth Army. A further blow to morale was the defeat at Stalingrad on January 31.

The Germans settled along a fortified line the French had constructed prior to 1940: the Mareth Line, the Tunisian "Maginot Line," on the heights behind the border with Libya. The British soon overran it, forcing the Germans to withdraw northward.

Regaining the initiative led to Operation *Frühlingswind* (*Spring Wind*) in February 1943. During a large outflanking operation, SdVbd.288 boldly secured a major objective: the Kasserine Pass, capturing the last Americans of the campaign.

The only mountain fighting 2./Pz.Gren-Rgt Afrika undertook in the North African campaign was brief. On March 31, Pz.Gren-Rgt Afrika was engaged to the south of Bou Hamra, facing an enemy thrust that had caused a crisis situation along the Gafsa–Gabès axis. The mountain company finally fell back on Enfidaville to dig in

A GJR756 soldier in Tunisia shows the strain. (GJR 765 Association)

Officers from GJR756 being briefed by their commander in the spring of 1943. The *Feldgrau Mantel* (greatcoat) was *de rigueur*.

and await inevitable capture by the French Foreign Legion. When Panzerarmee Afrika capitulated, most ex-Sonderverband 288 personnel in the Panzer-grenadier Regiment could not escape to Europe and were marched off into captivity.

Apart from a company-level unit included in a *Sonderverband*, a small two-battery mountain AA unit, the leichte Gebirgs-Flak-Abteilung 1, was engaged in North Africa as an organic unit of the Panzerarmee Afrika 1./ was annihilated at Tunis, and 2./ became 3./le.Flak-Abt. 760 in Italy. However, an experienced unit was needed for this more mountainous Tunisian terrain: Gebirgs-Jäger-Regiment 756.

Gebirgs-Jäger-Regiment 756

In November 1942, units assembled at Grafenwöhr camp in Bavaria in order to form a new infantry division of the *Kriemhilde* type, 334.ID under Major General Friedrich Weber. It would reinforce 5. Panzerarmee Colonel General von Arnim in North Africa following the American landings (Operation *Torch*). The division was made up of Inf.-Rgt754 and 755, and GJR756 whose commander, Lieutenant Colonel Arthur Hassels, had been awarded the Knight's Cross in Norway in 1940 at the head of II./GJR139. Recruits were given six weeks of training. Tropical dress was issued, except for the *Feldgrau* overcoats, the khaki model being unavailable. The division was one of the first to be equipped with MG 42 machine guns.

Fresh produce was bought from local traders. These NCOs from GJR756 bargain with a local farmer. The hatless *Oberfeldwebel* (master sergeant) in the background is wearing a French belt the wrong way round. (ECPAD)

A reenactor in GJR756 period dress with the grenade-launcher attachment on his weapon providing the characteristic silhouette not encountered in other theaters. (Private collection)

On December 20, 1942, troop movements between Grafenwöhr and southern Italy started with 21 days' issue of ammunition, supplies, and fuel. Troop trains crossed the Brenner Pass on Christmas Day. On the 27th, units disembarked at Nola to the east of Mount Vesuvius. The heavy matériel and the pack animals were separated from the troops, and transport to Tunisia via Sicily took three weeks, by sea to the port of La Goulette, and by air to Bizerte and El Aouina.

The division regrouped on January 3 in the Sidi-Athman sector. 334.ID set itself up defensively to the west of Tunis in the Sidi-Athman–Pont du Fahs, Chaouat and Tebourba sectors, under command of 10.PzD (Korpsgruppe Fischer) while waiting to be completely operational (declared as such on January 10). The division would return to this area each time it was put into reserve.

From January 15 onward, GJR756 was attached to Angriffsgruppe Weber (Colonel Weber's attack group), quickly renamed Kampfgruppe Weber, then on February 2, Korpsgruppe Weber. The composition of this battlegroup (or task force) changed depending on the missions it was given. Alongside various units equipped with heavy Tiger tanks, it took part in Operation *Eilbote I* (*Urgent Message I*) from February 16–25. These initial operations were aimed at reconquering the key points along the eastern crest—Kebir Pass, Nebana Defile, Oued Zarga, Djebel Bou Dabouss, Sbikha, and Goerat el Toubia—in order to maintain its capacity to react offensively and reestablish a coherent final defensive line facing west and southwest to help 5.Pz.Armee being gradually pushed back northward in Tunisia by the British from the south, and the Americans and the French from the west.

From January 28 to February 1, Kampfgruppe Weber took part in Operation *Eilbote II*, whose aim was recapturing ground lost to the Allies, with 11 Tigers and 14 Panzer IIIs, II./Pz.Gr.Rgt.69 and GJR756 forming the accompanying infantry. Leaving the Dra el Mamir region, the objective was Sbikha in Operation *Kuckucksei* (*Cuckoo's Egg*), on January 30/31, along the El Hamra Robaa road. However, aggressive antitank defense and dense minefields halted the Germans.

GJR756 was then engaged in the Djebel Mansour and Alliliga from February 3–5 against the 3rd French Foreign Legion Regiment (which lost its colors in the process) and a battalion from the British Parachute Regiment: it had to recapture the crest three times with heavy losses, about half its strength. In mid-February, the regiment's commander was seriously wounded; he was evacuated but died in Naples a few days later and was replaced by the CO of III./GJR756, Major Hörtnagl.

Among these prisoners from the Panzerarmee Afrika are several *Gebirgsjäger* wearing the edelweiss on their *Tropenmütze* (tropical caps) or recognizable by their *Bergschuhen* (mountain boots). The jerrycans, painted sand color, bear big white crosses, indicating that they are reserved for drinking water only. Different color variations in the *Zeltbahnen* (tent sheets or shelters) can be seen at the rear. (DR)

The *Kampfgruppe* attacked in the direction of Beja and Teboursouk during Operation *Ochsenkopf* (*Oxhead*), on February 26/27, to try and break the Allied encirclement. On this occasion, GJR756 was incorporated into Kampfgruppe Schmidt within the structure of Kampfgruppe Weber, with Jäger-Regiment Hermann Göring and an infantry battalion from 10.PzD.

From March 6–22, the division went back onto the defensive, carrying out reconnaissance missions toward the west. Fighting was bitter in the spring of 1943 and strategically agonizing for the Wehrmacht.

At the beginning of March, Kampfgruppe Weber was disbanded and GJR756 joined 334.ID. March was marked by particularly difficult living conditions, with execrable weather. The enemy *Jabos*—American P-38 Lightning and British Spitfire fighter-bombers—which the Germans were going to have to learn to live with, gave them no respite, especially in terms of supply vehicles, whereas off the coast the Royal Navy prevented any resupply by sea. By the end of the month, with Allied pressure mounting, the Panzerarmee Afrika and its operational area were quickly reduced. 334.ID resumed its defensive positions in its earlier rear echelon area.

On April 7, the final withdrawal of the division, whose strength had been systematically reduced, began to the west of Tunis, around Tébourba and Jedeida, toward Oued Medjerda. Strangely enough, until May 7, reinforcements kept arriving, enabling depleted units to be reconstituted, notably III. Bataillon that had been reduced to 15 or so men.

The division retreated one step at a time along Wadi Medjerba, up to the Bay of Tunis to the north of the town, and to the east along the Bizerte road. On May 8, the bulk of the division was encircled in the Mateur sector.

On May 9, GJR756 destroyed its weapons, its radios, and its vehicles and surrendered to the US 34th Infantry Division. It was never reconstituted as a mountain regiment and the number was attributed to an infantry regiment when 334.ID was reformed in Italy. The last units in Tunisia laid down their arms at Cap Bon and the German presence on African soil ended.

| The Eastern Front, 1942–45

Army Group South, Summer 1942–Summer 1943

Only two German mountain divisions (1. and 4.GDen) and one Romanian, without any army corps logistics units adapted to mountainous terrain and with no air transport, were made available to Army Group A (Field Marshal Wilhelm List), assembled for the conquest of the Caucasus, in Operation *Edelweiss*.

Additionally, XXXXIV.AK was sometimes called the Jägerkorps because at the time it included two divisions of *Jäger* (97. and 101., which had become *Jäger-Div.* on July 6 like all the *le.IDen*, or *leichte Infanterie-Divisionen*) suited to fighting in mountainous regions. These will be considered later. The three Italian mountain divisions followed in the second echelon. The southern wing of the 17. Armee, which had become Army Group Ruoff, comprising the LVII.PzK and XXXXIX.Geb.-AK, was given the mission (received on July 11) of attacking in the direction of Rostov.

On July 7, 1.GD, assigned to XI.AK, set off behind 295.ID, reinforced by Radfahr-Abt. Lawall as a *Vorausabteilung*. On the 21st, the division crossed the Donets at Kamensk, attached this time directly to Gruppe von Mackensen, then reached Rostov-on-Don at the beginning of August, without little fighting. There the division joined XXXXIX.Geb.-AK which it had left almost six months earlier.

A few days earlier, at the end of July, XXXXIX.Geb.-AK (four divisions, among which were 1. and 4.GDen) under *General der Gebirgstruppe* Rudolf Konrad, supported by IV. Fliegerkorps, had succeeded in forcing its way across the Don at its widest point, near its mouth at the Sea of Azov, thereby opening the way to the Caucasus. 1.GD joined the columns crossing the river. The operational areas were defined by the principal mountain range, the Caucasus: to the west of Mount Elbrus, the two GDen; to the east the 2nd Romanian Mountain Division. The overall objective was Tiflis (Tbilisi), across the Caucasus then along the Black Sea coast. Controlling the

Recovering local and regulation pack animals from the Red Army, the *Gebirgstruppen* discovered a new means of transport: the camel.

97.JgD, supported by panzers and Sturmgeschütze IIIs, approaches the foothills of the Caucasus. (Private collection)

three historical axes, called military roads (*Heerstraßen*, literally army roads) of Sukhumi, Georgia, and Ossetia was favored.

On July 9, Vorausabteilung Lawall in 1.GD reached the Kuban at Krapotkin and secured intact the bridges at Tcherkessk on the 11th. Elbrus could be seen from there. II./GJR98 (von Hirschfeld) began its approach to the Caucasus foothills that day at the confluence of the Kuban and the Teberda, encountering a strong Soviet rearguard. The *Vorausabteilung* took Teberda on the 14th before moving up along the valley of the same name. There it met the first Karatchaïs who welcomed them as liberators.[1] This was where the initial mountain fighting began, in the southwestern foothills of the Caucasus.

On August 17, Major Harald von Hirschfeld captured the Kluchor Pass (2,813 meters) fixing the Soviet resistance by making a frontal attack as a diversion, while destroying the enemy's rear and flanks by circumventing the mountain. Von Hirschfeld therefore held the only major road to Sukhumi. He was joined in the sector by Kampfgruppe Mayr from GJR99 (Colonel Kreß), on the Machar Pass, while the rest of GJR98 hurried to join von Hirschfeld in order to cover the right flank of the army corps.

As for XXXXIV.AK, it attacked toward Maykop, with its *Vorausabteilungen*, like Major Jordan's reinforced Radfahrabteilung 97 in the lead, followed by battlegroups from both JgRgt.204 and 206. The Soviet lines were breached in three places on the Belaya, on the Maykop–Apscherovskaya road, and in the Pschecha Valley.

Pi.Btl.97 formed a *Gefechtsgruppe* (similar to a battle group), incorporating the Legion Wallonie which had been assigned to the division in May for the attack on Schirvanskaya.

On the 21st, the German flag was planted on the summit of Mount Elbrus (5,642 meters) by the Hochgebirgs-Kompanie 1 under Captain Groth. Before that, the unit had reconnoitered several sites, glaciers, and high points. During the following days, the Dauner (the new commander of II./) and Hörl (III./) battalions from GJR99 relieved the Hochgebirgs-Kompanie Groth then dispatched reconnaissance missions southward. The imperial hunting lodge at Staryj Krugosor on the "King of the Caucasus," the Uschba (4,697 meters), changed hands several times.

After securing the area, the company settled into the lodge, where it found lots of supplies and mountain equipment. On the 19th and 20th, bad weather prevented an attempt

---

1 These Turkish-speaking peoples, descendants of the Alans, Islamized after Tamerlane's invasions in the 14th century and traditionally in revolt against the Russians, suffered particularly under the Bolshevik regime. Their collaboration with the Germans was the reason for mass deportations after the war. Some of them even drank to the health of Kaiser Wilhelm II—the Germans had indeed sent troops to support the Turks against the Russians in Georgia during the Great War.

1.GD progressing in the wooded Caucasus (*Waldkaukasus*), the valleys widening gradually and the vegetation disappearing.

Getting supplies to follow was a daily challenge, using men, or mechanical means like *Kettenkräder* (light tractors) and trailers, occasionally replacing the faithful *Mulis* (mules). (Franz Moll Archives)

on the summit. On the 21st at 1100 hours, 1. and 4.GDen unfurled the *Reichskriegsflagge* (Reich war flag) on the summit of Mount Elbrus, at 5,633 meters, the highest altitude reached by soldiers during World War II. This flag was removed by partisans in February 1943.

Of note is that that shortly before Groth's *Hochgebirgskompanie* was formed at 1.GD's initiative, the German command had set up a Hochgebirgsbataillon 1, mainly drawn from 1. Ausbildungsbataillon für Hochgebirgstruppen (1st Mountain Troops Instruction Battalion) at Berchtesgaden on July 20, 1942. This five-company battalion joined 1.GD as soon as it was ready to be distributed among the regiments. Hoch 1 was quickly disbanded and its personnel split up between the divisional regiments.

I./GJR99 and Radfahr-Abt. Lawall were reassigned, the former to the 2nd Romanian Division (1.PzA) and the latter to 13.PzD. In spite of the gradual arrival of reinforcements thrown into the battle as they came up,

The fighting in the Caucasus caused significant losses, where wounded soldiers were difficult to evacuate. (Private collection)

By the end of the summer of 1942, mountain divisions were recruiting *Hiwis* (*Hilfswilliger*, auxiliary volunteer) from prisoners and the local Karatchaïs. Some of them were regrouped into organic porter (*Gebirgsträger*) or cavalry units with special nationality insignias (inset) like this Cossack from *Bergkaukasien* (the mountain Caucasus). He is wearing a specific headdress, a Germanized *Kubanka*.

von Hirschfeld was trapped in the village of Klydisch. He had to face a strong northward enemy drive from the Maruschkoi Pass (2,790 meters) and go over to the defensive.

The Soviets had committed fresh troops, in particular a battalion made up of officer cadets from the school for mountain troops, a first for the Red Army. Normal infantry units in large numbers were also brought up in support.

At the end of August, the enemy started to move on the corps' western flank. Hochgebirgskompanie Schmidt (from Hoch 1 under Major Reisinger) protected the flank. In the valley of the Akssaut, pressure increased in front of Hoch 2, attacked on the 28th on the Maruschkoi Pass by a brigade consisting of a regiment of Georgian recruits, reinforced by a company only equipped with machine pistols, indicating that they were seeking close-quarter combat. 1.GD committed Kampfgruppe Eisgruber—I./GJR98 (Bader) and Art. Gruppe Grosse-Legge—to the pass, leaving the roads, scarce as they were, and attempting to envelop the enemy via the higher mountains (3,800–4,000 meters). The attack was halted on September 5. Hoch 2[2] under Major Paul Bauer distinguished itself by conquering the Kara-Kaya Mountains that day after a fierce struggle. But 1.GD, spread out over a 50-mile front and faced with fierce resistance, could not hope to continue its breakout to the Black Sea.

From August 23–30, 1942, pushing on to Sukhumi by the passes in the High Caucasus, 4.GD (Kampfgruppe von Stettner, II./GJR13 and III./GJR91), preceded by high-altitude patrols, took Mount Ssantscharo (2,592 meters), only a day's march from the Black Sea.

Mount Allichtrachu (2,726 meters) was captured on the 23rd, with Mount Tschamachara (2,055 meters) on the 26th, and Mount Ruland on the 28th also captured. A further operation enabled other passes to be taken: Adsapsch (2,579 meters) on September 8, Umpyrskij (2,500 meters) on October 4, and finally Psseaschcha (1,600 meters) on October 8 by the Enzian-Division, the "gentian" division.

But 4.GD, which had pushed on into the valley of the Bsyb, fell back on the Adsapsch Pass so that its forward elements would not be encircled. Indeed, the fact that XXXXIV. AK—the *Jägerkorps*, with its two divisions of *Jäger* (97. and 101.)—had halted at Tuapse in the forested regions of the North Caucasus (*Waldkaukasus*). With the Alpine divisions

---

2 Like Hoch 1, Hoch 2 was created on July 20, 1942 from II./AusB.-Btl für Hochgebirgstruppen at Innsbruck. It was also attached to 1.GD before becoming Gebirgsjäger-Bataillon 54 after having merged with Feldersatz-Bataillon 54 in February 1943. It then remained under command of 1.GD.

This "portrait" of a corporal enables us to appreciate the majesty of the Caucasus range.

The ascent up Mount Elbrus has started, the combat trains limited to the bare minimum. (Franz Moll Archives)

Conquering Mount Elbrus

On August 5, the day after crossing the Don, 1.GD ordered a *Hochgebirgs-Kompanie* (literally a high-mountain company) to be formed using the best mountaineers from the division and placed under Captain Groth. This temporary unit's mission was to capture the high passes in the Elbrus range and to run up the Reich flag, where, according to legend, Prometheus was chained. Groth was able to make an aerial reconnaissance of the range. Each of the participants (a hundred or so) was presented by the divisional commander with an eagle's feather to attach behind the edelweiss on his cap. It was a mission with symbolic meaning. The general staff didn't see the point but the division considered that this objective in its operational area was crucial. At the request of the army corps, ten men from 4.GD under Captain Gämmerle also took part in the operation.

On August 17, Groth made a reconnaissance of the passes on the main crest line: Chassan-Choï-Ssiurulgen (3,474 meters), Asau (3,260 meters), and Tschiper-Asau (3,268 meters), then Chotïu-Tau. Near this was the Elbrus Haus, a weather station perched at an altitude of 4,200 meters. Leaving his company ready to intervene, Groth entered the building alone, was taken prisoner but negotiated his release in return for the Russians being able to withdraw without loss and leaving the station as it was, which was accepted.

Not having a photograph of the conquest of the summit of Mount Elbrus, this is the *Reichskriegsflagge* used in other operational theaters. (DR)

This 7.5cm Geb.-Gesch 36 (left) has been installed at the highest artillery position of the war, at 4,400 meters, above the Elbrus Haus, the weather station. (*Signal*)

This first lieutenant (right) from Hochgebirgs-Kompanie Groth is wearing what's left of an eagle's feather fixed to his *Bergmütze* edelweiss. (*Signal*)

Colonel von Stettner, commander GJR91, seen here at a base camp in front of his tent, in the center, recognizable by the size of the peak of his cap and the height of his *Bergmütze*. He took command of 1.GD on January 4, 1943, and left the Caucasus for the Kuban. (Franz Moll Archives)

redirected to Stalingrad and the fact that it was impossible to ensure the logistics (carried by mules, losing 1,900 animals) in such a rugged region, the high command put a halt to the fighting in the High Caucasus on September 5. It hoped to resume the attack and reach the Black Sea by attacking between Maykop and Tuapse with three army corps.

1.GD left Gruppe Le Suire[3] on the main line of the crest and deployed to the Maykop region.

On September 10, Hitler himself took command of Army Group A.

3 Colonel Karl Hans von Le Suire, until then Dietl's chief of staff in Norway, had taken command of GJR99 on September 1, succeeding Kreß who took command of 4.GD and was promoted to major general on the same date. Kpf-Gr. Le Suire comprised GJR99, I./ and II./GAR79, as well as Geb.-A.A. 54 (Captain Mayr succeeding Major Lawall) and Geb.P.J.A.44 (Major Dr. Fahnler since May).

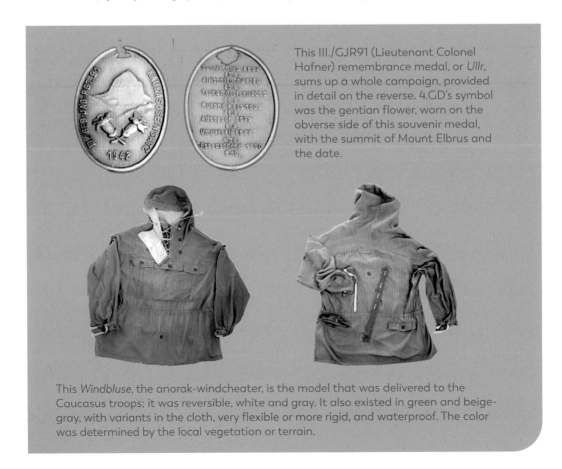

This III./GJR91 (Lieutenant Colonel Hafner) remembrance medal, or *Ullr*, sums up a whole campaign, provided in detail on the reverse. 4.GD's symbol was the gentian flower, worn on the obverse side of this souvenir medal, with the summit of Mount Elbrus and the date.

This *Windbluse*, the anorak-windcheater, is the model that was delivered to the Caucasus troops; it was reversible, white and gray. It also existed in green and beige-gray, with variants in the cloth, very flexible or more rigid, and waterproof. The color was determined by the local vegetation or terrain.

The first protective clothing against the weather reached XXXXIX.Geb.-AK at the end of 1942. Here a *Jäger* wears the *Windbluse* (jacket) and *Windhose* (trousers) at high altitude. (Franz Moll Archives)

The first MG 42s were issued during this period. The gun crew is wearing the *Windjacke*.

On October 10, Gruppe Lanz from XXXXIX.Geb.-AK, with 1.GD (whose Kampfgruppe Le Suire was guarding the southern flank) and part of 4.GD, guarded on the southeast flank by 46.ID (Major General Hacius), attacked toward the Black Sea on both sides of Tuapse, and took Schaumïan; but it was stopped 20 kilometers short of its objective. On its right, XXXXIV.AK attacked northward along the main road, and 97.JgD, reinforced by 7.(Geb.)/ Lehr-Rgt. Brandenburg, attacked along its eastern axis, ensuring contact was kept with Gruppe Lanz. The German attempt to break through continued until the beginning of November, then got bogged down, as the roads were being churned into quagmires, with supply lines and reinforcements unable to follow.

On October 28, Gruppe Lawall (built up around GJR98, whose group commander was awarded the Knight's Cross, and von Hirschfeld the Oak Leaves) captured Mount Ssmaschcho (1,036 meters), offering a promontory whence the Black Sea and the town of Tuapse could be seen. This was the furthermost point of the attack as particularly heavy fall rains made any movement almost impossible. Added to the weather, the troops were exhausted; subjected to extreme conditions, and having suffered heavy losses, this led to the advanced units falling back onto the main crest. Under pressure from the imminent catastrophe at Stalingrad, and after three months of delaying maneuvers, at the end of 1942 and the beginning of 1943, the corps settled on a 400-kilometer-wide defensive line running from the Caucasus Mountains to the Kuban where a bridgehead was established, ready for a possible withdrawal.

Gruppe von Le Suire thus joined 1.GD on January 27 after four months' separation and more than four weeks of falling back. The pack animal losses in 1.GD since it had arrived in the wooded Caucasus were colossal: 2,979 from exhaustion, 996 from enemy fire and 251 from sickness. At the head of 1.GD, Colonel Walter Stettner Ritter von Grabenhogen had taken over from Lanz on January 4. The division left the Caucasus for the *Goten-Stellung* (the

The gradual withdrawal from the Caucasus made the rearguard units all the more critical. This skier armed with a Gewehr 41 was drawn by Gisbert Palmié on propaganda cards. (Private collection)

Kampfgruppe von Le Suire (honored on the cover of *Die Wehrmacht*) gets ready to hold the line of the crest, here with a Geb.-Geschütz 36, This standard support weapon could be transported by mules, in eight loads, or drawn by two mules in harness, or directly with a towing hook by a *Kettenkrad*.

Gothic Line, not to be confused with the one in Italy, see the chapter "Italy, 1943–45"), the bridgehead on the Kuban, where it set itself up on February 1, 1943, with 4.GD to its south and 26.ID to its north.

From there, the corps began delaying maneuvers, backing onto defensive lines, *Hubertus-Stellung* (St. Hubert's Line) from February 5–10; February 21 *Diana-Stellung* (the Diana Line and the battle of Troitzkoya) and from February 22, *Poseidon-Stellung* (the Poseidon Line) backing on to the Sea of Azov. The withdrawal between these two lines was particularly trying as the snow and the mud concealed inundated paddy fields in which vehicles, horses, and sometimes complete baggage trains sank. On February 28, 1.GD was involved in heavy fighting around the lagoons bordering on the Sea of Azov, near Ssvistelnikov. In early March, severe weather prevented the Soviets, also literally bogged down in the mud, from carrying out an outflanking maneuver. The front was stabilized in mid-March.

But on March 22, 1943, 1.GD abruptly left XXXXIX. Geb.-AK for the Crimea. And from there, without stopping over, it headed for

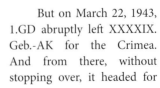

The fighting in the Kuban caused the *Gebirgstruppen* to link up with Romanian units engaged in the south of the Ukraine. Here a first lieutenant from the *Geb.-Pioniere* (right) poses with his Romanian counterpart. (DR)

These *Gebirgsjäger* found shelter in the Kuban Peninsula, recognizable by its thatched houses. (Franz Moll Archives)

Montenegro (see the chapter "The Balkans, 1942–45"). From mid-February, 97.JgD also fell back through successive lines of defense to the bridgehead on the Kuban where it settled to the southwest of Krasnodar. Heavy fighting ensued, in particular from the 4th to the 6th, and then on April 15/16 around Krimskaïa. 97.JgD cooperated for several months with Romanian units, some of which were subordinated to it.

The division reached the *Goten-Stellung* on May 12, facing an enemy who seemed determined to retake Novorossiysk. There was heavy fighting in this sector, until June 2, with four massive Soviet attacks following one another. The divisional commander, Ernst Rupp, lost his life on May 30. The days of in-depth offensive operations and *Vorausabteilungen* being deployed well in advance of the frontlines, had come to an end. Apart from several counteroffensives, the German armies never stopped retreating.

Army Group North, Summer 1942–Summer 1943

Following *Führerweisung* Nr. 41 (Führer directive No. 41), it was imperative to take up the "final" offensive against Leningrad again. Operation *Nordlicht* (*Northern Lights*)[4] was to start on September 14, 1942, under command of OB-11. Armee. Field Marshal Erich von Manstein, who had taken Sebastopol, the biggest citadel in the world, at the beginning of July, had just arrived with his five extra divisions. But the German project was unmasked—by the Red Orchestra spy network—and so the Soviets augmented

---

4 Not to be confused with the one in 1944, in Karelia, described in the following chapter.

A *Geb.-Beobachtungs-Abteilungen* observation balloon. Note the signaller in the foreground wearing *Windhose* and *Bergschuhe*. The nacelle is on the rear deck of the transport, with the balloon floating above it.

For moving around in the snow and ice, the mountain units used *akjas*, boat-like sledges painted white, that could carry reasonably heavy loads. The thaw seen here, occurring during the capture of this village, the houses of which are still burning, didn't make life any easier.

their strength with three armies comprising 20 divisions, nine brigades of fusiliers, and five armored brigades totaling 300 tanks, into the Volkhov sector. The objective the Russians defined for themselves for this second offensive (Operation *Sinyavino*) aimed at lifting the siege of Leningrad was a ravine between Lake Lagoda and the town of Mga—called the *Flaschenhals* (bottleneck) by the Germans and the "Shlisselburg-Sinyavino Cornice" by the Russians—in the direction of the Neva, with a massive concentration of forces.

The Soviets attacked first along the Leningrad Front on August 19—a few localized attacks—then across the Volkhov Front on the 27th, to the east and then the south of Sinyavino, preceding the German Operation *Nordlicht* by three weeks. The Germans, backing onto a saturated system of fortifications covered by artillery and mortar fire, were at first driven back but reacted with counterattacks that blocked the enemy, before coherently reforming their positions in a series of operations until October 15. The highest point, the strategic Sinyavino Heights, 150 meters above the surrounding plain, had remained "*in deutscher Hand*."

5.GD, under command of XXVIII.AK/18. Armee and initially held in reserve, was regrouped in order to mount a counterattack on August 27. GJR100 itself was attacked on the Neva between August 19–25. The division suffered heavy losses between September 10–20 and remained in reserve at the moment of the decisive counterattack launched on the 21st against Soviet forces already dug in defensively. But the Soviet advance to the south of Sinyavino degenerated into a pocket, encircled near Gaitlovo, and was gradually reduced by the Germans.

3.GD (Major General Hans Kreysing), subordinated to XXX.AK/11. Armee, arrived in August 1942 in Army Group North's sector as well, after several months' occupation in Norway. Until October 1, to the south of Shlisselburg, it took part in the defensive operations against the Soviet attempt to break the encirclement of the besieged town. The division found itself along the main Soviet axis of advance around Gaitlovo and suffered heavy losses, but reached the Mga region to reform.

The Soviet Sinyavino offensive eventually petered out and the Germans took advantage of it to fortify their positions in the bottleneck before the winter, digging trenches between the strongpoints. They finally received modern "very cold weather" equipment.

At the end of October, 3.GD was sent to the Velkiye Luki sector, on the boundary between Army Groups North and Center, where it had to get ready to leave for the Caucasus Front and Army Group A. But, on November 24, the Soviets attacked Velkiye Luki, upsetting the German defenses and penetrating several defensive positions by a few miles. Half the

A *Feldgrau* cap lined with natural fur (*Pelzmütze*). The bearer has affixed metal *Schirmmütze* insignia on the front and on the side a *Bergmütze* edelweiss.

division had already left by train; the remainder was disembarked and quickly engaged around Novosokolniki. GJR138, supported by GAR112, stopped the Russian advance at Tchenosiem, then counterattacked until November 26. However, GJR138 was surrounded by a Soviet counteroffensive, was almost annihilated and only a few survivors reached friendly lines.

On December 21, the other 3.GD units still on the move toward the Caucasus were halted so they could react to a crisis: the start of the Red Army's Operation *Saturn* aimed at the Italian 8th Army and the 2nd Romanian Division to the south of the Don, and therefore in the rear of Army Group South. At the same time, Operation *Uranus* was launched, the planned encirclement of the 6. Armee inside Stalingrad. Together, these operations would bring about the collapse of the whole southern part of the Eastern Front, or at least render any attempt to rescue the 6. Armee impossible. The Italian 8th Army was mostly destroyed.

GJR144 and other divisional units set themselves up in all-round defense at Millerovo from December 18. Soviet forces attacked on the 23rd, but were unable to take the town. On January 14, 1943, elements of 3.GD were ordered to fall back toward the Donets after destroying as many installations as possible and force their way through the Soviet encirclement. Gruppe Kreysing set itself up in a relatively quiet zone, to the southwest of Vorochilovgrad (Luhansk), under command of XXX.AK/1.Pz.Armee. The other divisional elements joined them during the latter part of March. 3.GD came under command of IV.AK (Lieutenant General Friedrich Mieth), of the new 6. Armee, on the banks of the Mius.

From January 12–30, 1943, after putting it off since December 1942 because the ice on Lake Lagoda and along the Neva was too thin, the Soviets launched Operation *Iskra* (*Spark*), aimed at relieving Leningrad which was still cut off, as was the Baltic fleet, from the rest of the Red Army, and destroying or at least significantly weakening Army Group North. *Iskra* was placed under command of Marshal Zhukov. 5.GD, initially in the army reserve (18. Armee, Colonel General Georg Lindemann) played a not unimportant role, but its regiments were spread out across different sectors.

The objectives in the bottleneck were more or less the same as during the preceding offensives, especially the Sinyavino Heights, which the Soviets attacked this time from the north, and therefore nearer Lake Lagoda. But the attack on the Volkhov Front (2nd Shock Army) took place at the same time as that against the Leningrad Front (67th and 8th Armies), respectively to the north and south of Gaitlovo. After a powerful preparatory artillery barrage at 0220 the two sides engaged. Pockets were created, counterattacked locally, and then attacked by the reserves.

GJR85 was split up into battalions in the Shlisselburg sector. The rest of 5.GD was in reserve in the Mga region, organized in *Kampfgruppen* so as to be capable of reacting to any breakthroughs.

On January 18, the German defenders were forced to abandon Shlisselburg, leaving their heavy matériel behind before arriving south of Sinyavino. The siege of Leningrad was

On the cover of *Die Wehrmacht*, an MG has been placed on the edge of the trench. The *Jäger* are waiting for the next attack, living in appalling conditions.

partially lifted. The Soviets immediately started building a railway to supply the city, even though the corridor was narrow and within range of the German artillery. It would take a new year and several more offensives to completely lift the siege of the metropolis of the north once and for all. At the same time, Stalingrad fell in the south, and the Demyansk and Rzhev (Rschew) pockets had to be abandoned in the north, the beginning of 1943 marking a strategic turning point.

In March, with a high point from the 19th onward, the Soviets launched the second battle of Lagoda, before the thaw. This came at the beginning of April and quickly the two belligerents, literally, got bogged down without any significant successes but with heavy losses.

Army Groups South, North Ukraine, and South Ukraine, Summer 1943–Summer 1944

Gebirgstruppen were represented in the Army Group South sector, greatly contested by the major units which had fallen back from the Caucasus: 4.GD from XXXXIX.Geb.-AK, 97. and 101.JgDen in the XXXXIX. Jägerkorps. These two *bergfähig* (mountain-proficient) divisions of *Jäger* were given extra training, the same mountain training as the *GDen* had already been given. In July 97.JgD continued in defense in the South Kuban with an effort around Moldavskoya.

The Soviet attacks followed one after the other throughout the month, and in August, then tailed off until the beginning of September. On September 14, the division started to fall back west, along the Taman Peninsula, through successive lines starting with the *kleine Goten-Stellung* (Little Gothic Line).

In fall of 1943, the Eastern Front was thus realigned on Mariopol (Zhdanov)–Dnieper–Vitebsk. 17. Armee and its V, XXXXIV.Geb.-AK and XXXXIV.AK. abandoned the Kuban bridgehead (also called *Gotenkopf*, Goth's head). XXXXIX.Geb.-AK was engaged on the left-hand flank of the army in a lagoon region.

Indeed, in September the withdrawal toward the Crimea became more apparent. XXXXIX.Geb.-AK was given the task of bringing up the rear, evacuating the last six divisions engaged. GJR13 (4.GD), the last unit to cross the Kerch Straits on the way back, closed the door on October 9, leaving no weapons or vehicles on the eastern bank. The Soviets tried several times to infiltrate behind the German lines but were driven off each time with heavy losses. The corps chief of staff (Colonel Michael) and three of his divisional commanders were killed during this withdrawal: Haccius (46.ID), Schmitt (50.ID), and Kreß (4.GD).

This situation once again illustrated how the German COs characteristically commanded from the front; the death of General Ernst Rupp, commander of 97.JgD (XXXXIV. Jägerkorps) in the lower Kuban, mentioned earlier, being a case in point.

XXXXIX.Geb.-AK took command of most of the Crimean Peninsula. The general commanding organized his defense around the Sevastopol "fortress," a rather pompous term designating the fortified strongpoints that had been seriously damaged in 1941, and the wrecked port installations—and the three lines of defense between Sivash Bay and Sevastopol, aimed at preventing a Soviet breakthrough from the north. Among the major units engaged in Crimea was the two-division Romanian Mountain Corps, under command of General Schwab, a Saxon from Transylvania (Siebenbürgen in German) and former World War I Austro-Hungarian officer.

In October, after it emerged from the Kuban bridgehead, 4.GD was transferred to the (new) 6. Armee which, from the northeast of the Crimea, had to contain the Soviet drive toward Odessa and Nikopol. The front stabilized during the winter. The Soviets attacked with great determination on the Perekop Isthmus on April 8 and May 12, 1944, and after a month of fighting for the Crimea, Sevastopol fell. As Hitler had refused to allow German and Romanian units to withdraw, the result was heavy losses in troops and matériel, especially among the isolated units. Still under command of 6. Armee, 4.GD continued to fall back and set up its positions on the Dniester and the Bug.

The battle of Kursk—Operation *Zitadelle* (*Citadel*)—had broken out farther north on July 5, 1943. 1.Pz.Armee and 6. Armee, which made up the frontline of Army Group South, were ordered to carry out offensive operations. But the Soviets launched a big offensive on the Donets and the Mius which the Germans were only able to stop on the 30th. 3.GD, in a sector far from the main Soviet thrust, sent temporary reinforcements (GJR144) to neighboring 304.ID.

On August 16, the Soviet Southwestern Front, followed on the 19th by the Southern Front, attacked in turn in the Donets Basin and forced the divisions engaged there to retreat westward. Major General Georg Picker, commander 3.GD, gathered together the reserve units in the sector—five infantry battalions, six artillery batteries, one *Stug-Batterie* and two antitank companies—and in order to relieve XVII.AK attacked on its southern front, and counterattacked southward into the flank of the 5th Shock Army, which had succeeded in opening a breach between the Mius and the Krynka through which Red Army units poured en masse.

This counterattack on the flank elicited a powerful Soviet response and in spite of destroying 84 enemy tanks, Gruppe Picker was forced to withdraw on August 21.

IV.AK, together with 17.PzD and 3.GD, made up a force enabling them to counterattack north–south to halt the Soviet breakthrough. On August 30, 3.GD had reached the Kuteinikovo region. Against the advice of Field Marshal von Manstein, which he had given at Vinnitsa, Army Group South's HQ, Hitler wanted to hold on to the Donets Basin. However, faced with enemy pressure, on his own initiative, Manstein ordered the entire army group to withdraw westward, backing onto prepared intermediary lines or watercourses, up to the Dnieper. In August, orders were given to make the river a major obstacle, the *Ostwall*, the East Wall, equivalent of the Atlantic *Westwall*. The Russians entered Stalino on September 7 and the Donets Basin was in their hands.

3.GD (Major General Wittmann) firstly withdrew to the *Eidechsenstellung* (Lizard Line) on September 9 in the Antonovka sector then onto Gaitschul on the 14th and Konk on the 16th. Finally, almost without stopping, it reached the *Wotanstellung*, in front of the

The Kuban Peninsula was littered with lagoons. The *Jäger* were given the nickname of *Sumpfjäger*, marsh hunters. The quickest way of getting around was quite often by boat, generally requisitioned. This time the uniforms of these *Jäger* laying telephone lines is khaki. They have reinforced their firepower with a Soviet PPSh 41 machine pistol.

Ostwall, on the 20th. This respite was short lived: the Soviets reached the *Wotanstellung* on September 26 and attacked immediately. The Knight's Cross was awarded to three men from GJR138 during this four-day battle The enemy resumed the attack on October 9, and later, on November 14–20. When it was over, 3.GD had reached the bridgehead at Nikopol to the east of the Dnieper. Hitler wanted to retain this region which was rich in iron and manganese deposits, and beyond it, the great Nogaic steppes stretched away, so favorable for armored operations.

97.JgD had been established in the Nikopol bridgehead since the beginning of November, given a line of defense over flat terrain and without any significant settlements in the area; the freezing weather had already appeared and made digging trenches and shelters very difficult. The division held fast against continuous Soviet infantry and armor attacks from the end of November to Christmas.

On January 12, 1944, the Russians launched a winter offensive against the Nikopol bridgehead, and after a massive attack from the north along the river, forced 97.JgD to retreat across the Dnieper at Bolshaya Lepetikha in appalling conditions, on February 8. During its three months in this sector, the division had driven off five major attacks. Evacuating the sector right in the middle of the early thaw and therefore on very impracticable terrain, with heavy rains, liquid mud and peat bogs, and under constant pressure from the enemy, caused the Germans heavy matériel losses.

A withdrawal for 97.JgD to benefit the *Jägerkorps* in Crimea had already been envisaged but Major General Ferdinand Schörner, BefH Hgr., had refused; however, pressure from the Soviets decided otherwise and 3.GD fell back to the west of the Dnieper on February 12 to relieve 97.JgD on the 14th after it had just counterattacked northward at Bolschaya Kostromka.

On February 18, another wave of cold weather (14°F) hardened the ground in the region. 3.GD on the orders of XXIX.AK settled farther north on the Inguletsz in the Krasnyj–Micolayev region—where it held fast against powerful attacks—until March 13. At the same time, under command of XXIX.AK, 97.JgD counterattacked the enemy flank (39th Fusilier Regiment of the Guard) northwestward and parallel to the Micolayev–Novyi Bug railway line. Outflanked by powerful enemy forces, the division had to break off and force its way through to the Bug on the 18th.

After skirmishes from March 18–27 against a Soviet bridgehead on the Bug, the division followed

At the same time as the sleeve escutcheon was introduced, and like the *Gebirgstruppen* system, a metal cap insignia, the *Eichenlaubbruch* (oak leaves sprig) was introduced with the same symbolism as the sleeve escutcheon.

This *Jäger* captain in Crimea in the spring of 1944 is wearing "half-season" (note that canvas used for tents cannot be lightweight) dress, with a jacket cut from heavy canvas, no doubt Russian, with a collar made of blue-green cloth and all the insignia of his arm.

The escutcheon sewn on the jacket sleeve is the troops' model; created on October 2, 1942, it was introduced gradually from the spring of 1943 onward. It is shown here in closeup.

Operation *Alphabet*, a withdrawal in 12 days over 300 kilometers up to the Dniester. All that was left of 3.GD after this withdrawal through successive lines was the equivalent of a regimental *Kampfgruppe*, which withdrew again at the beginning of June to the Moldava, in the Draceni region. 97.JgD set itself up on either side of Talmaz, under command of LII.AK. By March 19, Operation *Margarethe* had put Hungary under German control. In April, the Russians had reached Galicia and the north of Bessarabia, and were already driving toward Moldavia. The risk of Romania then Hungary defecting was becoming more likely.

On April 1, 1944, given the operational situation, Army Group South split into Army Group North Ukraine and Army Group South Ukraine.

On April 17, XXIX.AK authorized 3.GD to fall back so it could consolidate. The corps had a *Feuerwehr*—a "fire brigade"—Kampfgruppe GJR138, which it engaged as a mobile reserve and which again suffered heavy losses before it returned to the division on May 28. Meanwhile, the rest of 3.GD was given a sector to defend in the Talmaz region, where it was calm enough to incorporate 2,500 extra troops and to attach Kampfgruppe Höhne from 97.JgD.

On May 22, 3.GD left its positions and reached the foothills of the eastern Carpathians, to the south of Tchernivtsi, under command of XVII.AK. The division was assigned Romanian elements as well as marching battalions, increasing its operational capacity.

Army Group North, Summer 1943–Summer 1944

The third battle of Lagoda began on July 2, 1943. Two Soviet armies attempted to secure the Leningrad–Kirishi railway line. But once again they ran into German divisions solidly dug in, and by the end of September, this new offensive was halted. The Saviniano Heights and the railway line remained, once again, "*in deutscher Hand*." 5.GD, positioned on the *Mga-Stellung*, went through a period of particularly harsh fighting, typical of this war of position: along a 74-kilometer front, 1,872 strongpoints had been built, echeloned in depth, separated by zones of interlocking fire and obstacles. 5.GD was moved to the Italian Front in December 1943 (see later chapter "Italy, 1943–45") where Allied progress was causing concern. The mountain units were no longer engaged with Army Group North and so did not experience the winter offensive the Soviets launched in January to finally break the Leningrad siege. Note, however, the presence of 28.JgD in this northern sector, whose artillery regiment became GAR28 on February 20, 1944, with the infantry units remaining *Jäger*.

Army Group Center, Summer 1944–Spring 1945

The Soviet summer offensive, Operation *Bagration*, that commenced in June 1944, was to decide the outcome of the war once and for all; the primary effort was made against Army Group Center, which had fallen back on *Panther-Stellung*. The mountain units only felt the repercussions of this large-scale operation which erased more than 20 divisions from the Wehrmacht's order of battle. The Red Army was to reach the borders of the Reich in the north, in East Prussia.

Few units in the subject of our study were engaged full time in the Army Group Center sector. Battalions of skiers were regrouped into a brigade then into a division of *Skijäger*, and were engaged farther south where Army Group Center and Army Group South merged, in particular during the big Soviet summer offensive.

The *Skijäger* were attached to the *Gebirgstruppen* for several reasons: they had inherited the traditions of the *Schneeschuhtruppen*, the skiers of the Great War who became the Alpine troops then the mountain troops within the Alpenkorps and the Karpatenkorps; skiing at the beginning of World War II was almost exclusively limited to the mountain troops and a number of their battalions trained ski battalions during the first winter out east, then made up the kernel of a brigade then a division and finally, the *Skijäger* Association was attached to the Federation of German Mountain Troop Associations.

From September 1941, two-week courses were organized for the units of the *Ostheer*— the "land" component in the East—with the support of Finnish officers who shared their experience of the Winter War against the Soviets. Instruction was on the impact of winter on operational functions, including combat, movement, logistics, and preserving personnel and matériel. The order to set up the battalion of skiers was promulgated on December 12, 1941 by Field Marshal Günther von Kluge, Oberkommando (OB) Army Group Center.

The first winter on the Eastern Front turned out to be very harsh indeed for the units only equipped for a summer or half-season war. The temperatures went down to -49°F or even -58°F in certain sectors. By December 1, 1941, the *Ostheer* had already lost 24 percent of its potential, facing an adversary who was indeed weakened but who had inexhaustible human resources, among which were 34 divisions from Siberia, particularly suited to a winter war.

Withdrawn to the Kursk–Rzhev line, Army Group Center faced a Soviet counterattack which broke through to the north of Smolensk in the Velikiya Luki sector. The *Winterkampfschulen* (winter warfare schools) at Gschatzk and Orel, supported by the *Heeres-Hochgebirgsschule Fulpmes* (the "high-mountain school of the Army" located in the Stubai valley in the Tyrol), constituted the first skier unit, placed under command of Major Hans von Schlebrügge, a *Gebirgsjäger*. Personnel were recruited from several units and included a number of champions like Gustl Berauer,

Observation posts were installed in watchtowers made of wood and reeds; this one surmounts a bunker made of stone and logs. (Lenz Archives)

mentioned in *German Mountain Troops 1939–42* (1.GD, summer 1941). The battalion naturally was initially called Ski-Bataillon Schlebrügge (SBS), then later Jäger-Bataillon 3. It consisted of a *Stabs-Kp.*, and four combat companies one of which was a heavy company.

Declared operational on January 7, 1942, the SBS had its baptism of fire over the next few days, to the east of Smolensk, where 4. Armee (Kübler) to the north and 2.PzArmee (Schmidt) merged, between Jucknow to the north and Spas-Demensk, along a major logistics route. The *Skijäger* were confronted in -47°F conditions by aggressive Siberian troops as well as by paratroopers dropped behind the German lines encircling the battalion.[5] Schlebrügge was seriously wounded in the initial skirmish and his adjutant, First Lieutenant Hett, took command of the battalion. In February and March, the SBS opposed several breakthroughs in the 50-kilometer-wide zone in which it was engaged, using its platoon of mounted Cossacks (*skijoring*, being pulled on skis), its Panzer and Sturmgeschützen, both at night and by day. The *rasputitsa*, the thaw, in April didn't spare the skiers who found it more difficult to get around.

The need to organize these units into *Jagdkommandos* quickly became evident. The *Jäger* stayed out for a week at a time, sometimes without seeing a house, in temperatures that plunged to -56°F, which even for the Russians caused terrible frostbite, death from pneumonia, and extreme hypothermia in the wounded who were extremely difficult to move quickly enough in order to survive. The way the *Skijäger* put up with these extreme conditions was considered superhuman.

The appellation *Jagdkommando* was taken up to designate other units: Jago 1 (Jagdkommando 1, Major von Renois) with three companies, reached the front at the end of January, as did Skijagdkommando 7 which was soon engaged in the direction of Velkiye Luki. The next *Jagos* were quickly made up in late December/early January and sent to the front: Jago 3 (Berlin, three *Kp.*), Jago 4 (Dresden, three *Kp.*), Jago 5 (Stuttgart, three *Kp.*), Jago 6 (Münster, three *Kp*), Jago 8 (Salzburg, two *Kp* and one *M.G-Kp.*), Jago 9 (Salzburg), Jago 11 (Magdeburg), and Jago 12 (Luxembourg/Baumholder, 4 *Kp.*). Besides, 2.GD equipped III./GJR136 (Captain Stampfer) so it could be mobile on the snow, and 7.GD helped Ski-Batallion 82 to get established.

Finally, each Luftflotte organized a battalion of Luftwaffe skiers. Like the SBS, which became Jäger-Btl.7, the other *Jagos* became *Jagd-Btle* with the coming of summer, usually acquiring a heavy company on the way, and were engaged on the front's hotspots. During the summer, 12 Jagd-Bataillone was constituted at Arys, East Prussia, from existing *Jagos* and new recruits. A 13th followed, as well as a 14th in fall 1943, which existed as such for only a few weeks.

These units were engaged as light infantry on the front in the summer and suffered extremely high losses—1./Jäger 3 lost 16 company commanders in three months—in particular around Velikiya Luki and its fortifications, the "marsh fortress," which were pounded throughout the summer by Soviet artillery to soften up the defenders, before being attacked at the end of December. Reinforcements in men, matériel, and supplies were brought in by gliders but few soldiers succeeded in escaping encirclement, despite attempts to break out in mid-January. Other battalions participated in the battles of Orel, Vitebsk, Gomel, Briansk, Viazma, Smolensk, Rhzev, Nevel, Novgorod, Kholm, and Velisch. Once

---

5 These Soviet troops were dropped without parachutes from a height of 10 meters. In spite of the relative cushioning effect of the snow, only 50 percent were left fit for combat, and this took place in front of the German firing positions.

During operations in the Nikopol bridgehead between November 1943 and February 1944, 3.GD and 97.JgD were engaged in fierce fighting, suffering heavy losses. The NCO checking the mail and the *Jäger* on his left are wearing reversible white/green, padded, fleece-lined jackets. The cap has an uncommon single button as, apparently, headdress insignia had not as yet been received. (DR)

they were back up to strength, Jäger-Btle.3 and 6 deployed to Finland.

Jäger-Btl.3, the kernel of GJR856, set up with marching units a few days before Norway capitulated, a unit far removed from the big centers, only laid down its arms several weeks after the end of hostilities.

Following the measures promulgated by HQ during the summer for regrouping units, constituting Ski-Jäger-Brigade 1 was formalized on August 8, 1943, as were the terms designating the other units: Ski-Jäger-Brigade (SJB), Ski-Jäger-Regiment (SJR), Ski-Jäger-Bataillon (SJBtl), Schweres-Ski-Bataillon (SSB), Ski-Pionier-Bataillon (SPB), Ski-Nachrichten-Abteilung (SNA), Ski-Fernsprech- and Ski-Funk-Kompanie (SFFK), and Ski-Feldersatz-Kp. (SFK).

The brigade and regimental levels were represented by headquarters and a *Stabs-Kp*, to command four *SJBtl* and one *SSB*. The antitank components, indirect support (motorized heavy howitzer, artillery), Flak, heavy mortars, Sturmgeschützen, snow ploughs, war dogs and sledge dogs, gradually started to arrive. One of the two transport companies was equipped with Maultier Sd.Kfz. 3 half-tracks. The heavy matériel was self-propelled.

The infantry component was made up around two regiments, SJR1 (Colonel Weiler) and 2 (Major von Salisch). The date for the end of preparations was put back several times and was then fixed once and for all at January 12, 1944. The question had been raised of how to use this new, highly mobile brigade with a lot of heavy firepower. Army Group Center, which had supplied almost all the elements enabling this major unit to be assembled, had no intention of letting go of it, and deployed it for its baptism of fire in a critical sector, to the south of 2. Armee (Weiss) and more particularly XXIII.AK, on the Pripyat.

The first elements (1./SJR1, Captain Meergans) were moved forward in Junkers Ju 52s and intervened on January 14 in the morning. Reinforced by quadruple-2cm gun carriages on half-tracks, they drove off a Russian attack. The rest of the brigade gradually joined it and took over a 63-kilometer-wide front along the Pripyat River.

The *Skijäger* were disappointed: for their first engagement, some units reached areas where a warm spell was taking place, with no snow, but with impressive potholes. (A vet reported seeing a *Gulaschkanone* (field kitchen) disappear completely to one of these craters with its team of two horses.) The positions the brigade occupied backed onto strongpoints (*Stützpunkte*) to the north of the river—SJR1 to the east—from which *Kampfgruppen*, forward positions, and close-in patrols could act as *Jagdkommandos* up to 20 kilometers from the *HKL* (*Hauptkampflinie*, literally main combat line, i.e., the front). By the end of January, the brigade had broadened the bridgeheads by 15 kilometers, to the south of the Pripyat, at Gorki, Ossmalenik, and Samoschia.

They also supported major neighboring units, like 5.PzD to the north of the Pripyat, with 2./SJR2 and the 3rd StuG Battery. Supporting fire was difficult to institute in these marshy areas. A typical operation occurred on January 25 when a *Jagdkommando* from Meergans' battalion slipped through onto a Russian artillery battery, in position 12 kilometers away, harassing the regiment; they neutralized it, luckily without running into any partisan groups that infested the region.

However, after a few skirmishes with significant losses, but above all because of the absolutely execrable weather conditions (melting snow, three-meter-deep potholes) seriously interfering with mobility and evacuating the wounded, the brigade fell back on its *HKL* between February 2–5. (The *Skijäger* gave themselves the name "*Schlammjäger*," literally "muddy Jäger.") The winter weather then returned, making movement easier.

On March 19, with significant Stuka support, 1. and 2./SJR2 reclaimed the village of Betschi which two Soviet battalions had taken earlier, a few kilometers to the south of the *HKL*. At the end of March, part of SJR2 was sent to its western neighbor, 7.ID., as a reinforcement. The units suffered heavy losses and were threatened with encirclement.

By the end of March, as the Soviets reached Kovel, aiming for Brest-Litovsk, 2. Armee mounted an operation to break out, and dispatched SJB1 300 kilometers from its positions on the Pripyat, to the southwest of Kovel, under command of LVI.PzK (Gruppe Hossbach). The Wiking Division (5. SS-Panzer-Division, General Gille) had indeed retaken Kovel on April 4, but was surrounded there. The brigade arrived in the area on April 13, and the next day took Stavki, 40 kilometers southeast of Kovel, near the Turja River, where elements (only SJR2 had arrived almost whole) advanced along the banks during the night of the 15th/16th. The brigade was reinforced with Hungarian elements and carried out an offensive reconnaissance operation toward the southwest with Kampfgruppe Rast (commander of Ski. PiBtl.1). Continuing this return to offensive operations—after skirmishing with Soviet units dug in in defense and with unlimited fire support—Operation *Ilse* (retaking the western bank of the Turja between Kovel and Turyisk) opened on April 27, and lasted a week. Losses were heavy, especially among the officers.

On May 13, 1944, Colonel Martin Berg, a 39-year-old holder of the Knight's Cross, took command of SJB1 during a period of relative calm, though all felt it was the calm before the storm. On June 2, the brigade became 1.Ski-Jäger-Division (1.SJD), but it only received each of its *SJR*s and the third group of the *SAR* later. On June 13, 1.SJD was put on alert at its position along the Turja, spread out as far as Kovel.

On June 23, 1944, to support the Anglo-American landings in Normandy, the Soviets launched Operation *Bagration*, their big summer offensive. The thrust was against Army Group Center (Field Marshal Busch, then Model after June 28), along 1,100 kilometers between the Pripyat marshes and the Düna. In four weeks, 23 out of the 40 divisions of the German army group were annihilated, creating a 450-kilometer breach which the Russians poured through. This attack was halted in the northeast, in front of Riga, behind Army Group North (Colonel General Lindemann, then Friessner after July 3, and Schörner after July 23). Liaison with Army Group Center was therefore uninterrupted. To the south, the Army Group Center–Army Group North Ukraine junction remained intact. 1.SJD held its positions along the Turja until mid-July, facing Red Army units that no doubt had been given the task of fixing it there.

The insignia adopted in June 1944, confirmed in September, in the Skijäger-Brigade (then Division) comprised a cap insignia: the *Jäger* model at first barred with a ski cut out of cartridge cases and soldered, then made from a single stamped piece; and a BEVo woven (embroidered for the officers) sleeve escutcheon: the *Jäger* model, barred with two white crossed skis; the epaulettes bore the regimental number, the brigade being originally considered as *Heerestruppe*, with a pale green loop (*Schlaufe*) in the SJR1. (Private collections)

But on July 16, the Army Group North Ukraine front was penetrated in turn in Poland and in Galicia. On the 18th, a breakthrough by Soviet armor in the neighboring sector and thunderous artillery barrages forced SJR 1 to start partially falling back in order to avoid an attack in its rear, followed by the rest of the division the next night—it was now a race against the enemy—relying as much as possible on the friendly lie of the land. On the 21st, the division crossed over to the west of the Bug, the bridges of which were congested, with the Soviets snapping at the rearguard's heels.

On August 1, after delaying operations and after abandoning large quantities of heavy matériel and combat trains, the last 1.SJD elements broke through the Soviet units along the river and crossed over to the western bank of the Vistula (Weichsel) at Annopol, where the division dug in. Their arrival in the sector was marked by particularly costly fighting for control of an island on the river, to the north of Annopol. The Russians even tried to swim across the river.

On August 1, 1944, the Warsaw uprising erupted at the call of the Resistance leader, General Bor-Komorowski, in the hope that the Soviets, who had reached the Vistula, would intervene and help them. Nothing happened: the Russians stayed put, doing nothing, or at least not doing anything to assist the uprising. Several Wehrmacht units using foreign recruits, including mountain units, were engaged (see Sonderverband Bergmann in *German Mountain Troops 1939–42* and Ski-Bataillon Norge at the end of the "Norway and Finland, 1942–45" chapter in this volume). The insurgents were obliged to capitulate on September 2.

Until August 7, the Soviets tried to cross the Vistula in the 1.SJD sector. On the 8th, breaking out of the bridgehead they had created on the river at Baranow Sandomierski, they advanced north, outflanking the division using elements which were driven off by Ski-Feld-Ersatz-Bataillon 1. On the 17th, the Soviets resumed their attack to extend the bridgehead to the south of Annopol and outflank 1.SJD in the rear, again unsuccessfully, just as on the 22nd, but with extra means.

The end of Operation *Bagration* was fixed for August 19. After the Ukraine, Byelorussia was liberated, as was a part of Poland. On the 23rd, Romania's defection left an enormous breach in the German positions. The Soviet assaults on the Vistula continued. 97.JgD found itself almost shoulder to shoulder with 1.SJD facing the Baranow bridgehead which it succeeded in reducing by taking it in a vise with 4.PzD and 16.PzD between August 26 and September 1.

During the night of the 2nd/3rd, leaving two battalions with XXXXVIII.AK temporarily to the east of Ostrowiec, 1.SJD was withdrawn from the Vistula and sent northwest, to the wooded heights of the Lysa Gora ridge, in the Kielce region, under command of XXXXII. AK. The division stayed only until September 22, involved mainly in artillery duels, before urgent deployment to the eastern Beskides Mountains, on the border between Poland and Slovakia on the Carpathian, Dukla, and Ozenna passes, to face the 4th Ukrainian Front (Rokossovsky) and the 38th Army of the 1st Ukrainian Front (Konev).

The Soviets aimed to link up with the Slovakian insurgents who had turned on Germany at the end of August at Banska Bystrica. They launched their attack on September 8. The first elements of 1.SJD arrived on the 24th and attacked on the 25th, under command of the new divisional commander Major General Gustav Hundt. With terrible artillery barrages, and right in the middle of the woods, a Soviet cavalry attack materialized. Few cavalrymen survived.

Facing 1.SJD were the Soviet 38th Army and elements of the Czech I Army Corps, supported by the Red Air Force and its fearsome Ilyushin Il-2 Sturmoviks, nicknamed the *Fliegende Panzer* (flying tank). The Russians attacked without letting up, but without succeeding in breaking through in spite of using tanks—which struggled in the wooded and uneven terrain—and failing to force the division to fall back from the Ozenna pass after abandoning the pass at Dukla.

During the first three weeks of October, I./SJR1 thus sustained 56 attacks at all levels. The Kapisova Valley, between Dukla and Ozenna, was nicknamed the "valley of death," where hundreds of tank carcasses remained for years. At the end of October, the division reported that enemy pressure had decreased because the Russians were trying to wear them down with artillery barrages and patrols rather than large infantry and tank attacks. During the night of October 27/28, the Slovak high command ordered its units to join the Soviet resistance.

The stability of the front along the *Gisela-Stellung*—in the process of being reorganized—enabled 1.SJD to make up its numbers and create a new unit, the schnelles Ski-Jäger-Bataillon. The division stayed in this relatively quiet sector until the beginning of December and the arrival of torrential rains. On the 12th, its half-track Flak 37 company was sent to reinforce XXXXIX.Geb.-AK. On December 16, the rest of the division was ordered to join this mountain corps on the southern and northern approaches to Kosice (Kaschau), 80 kilometers to the south of its positions where the Hungarian front had collapsed.

97.JgD was its northeastern neighbor. On very uneven and undulating terrain, the division found itself fighting against Romanians alongside their Russian allies. From December 18 to the end of the month, SJR1 was engaged in heavy fighting toward Bodollo, 20 or so kilometers southwest of Kosice, against aggressive Romanians. I./GJR13 from 4.GD was sent to reinforce the division in the Torna sector. On December 24, after several days of fierce fighting, companies from III./SJR1 (Major Schülke), backed by accompanying Sturmgeschütz platoons, took Torna. Company strength was melting away, while the Germans still had to hold on to disproportionately large swaths of territory once they went over to the defensive.

On the same day a Hungarian "counter-government" declared war against Germany from Debrecen. But the Hungarian 1st Army under General Lazlo remained faithful to the Germans and received 3. and 4.GDen as reinforcements, with the latter in position to the west of Torna. From January 10–17, 1945, the Soviets launched a massive attack against Bodollo and forced the division to fall back and abandon Košice, then to withdraw unit by unit from January 20 onward, toward Upper Silesia, because of the pressure of events in the neighboring sectors.

These *Skijäger* from SJR1 are wearing characteristic clothing: *Feldgrau* Panzer wraps, canvas belts painted white, and paratrooper helmets; during the icy winter of 1944/5, in particular, they wore fleece-lined items.

The Russians had indeed already broken through into this province in depth to over 200 kilometers. To the north of XXXXIX.Geb.-AK. Army Group Heinrici had improvised lines of defense with marching units and *Volkssturm*; nonetheless, it had to pull its units back westward along the valley of the Waag, to the south of Krakow, by road and rail. Soviet partisans, commanded by regular officers, harassed the units in their rear, in particular the support units. Most of the populace refused to flee west, even though they were aware of the fate reserved for civilians: death, rape, and pillage.

On January 22, 1945, the Soviets set up several bridgeheads to the west of the frozen Oder, only encountering limited resistance in the Oppeln–Brieg–Ohlau region. 97.JgD, still engaged in the Košice sector, under XXXXVIII.AK, sustained strong enemy attacks. On the 23rd, 1.SJD, reinforced by 8.8cm AA cannon (Luftwaffen-Flak-Abteilung I./33) positioned itself 60 or so kilometers to the west of Košice, immediately to the east of the Oder, around Rybnik. The other bank was held by 8.PzD, at Raciborz. In fact, because of the terrain and the enemy threat, the two divisions were in places interlocked. 97.JgD set up to the south of Racibórz then sent units to other divisions north and northeast of the town at the beginning of February.

On January 25, the Soviets attacked the division and broke through in depth, the *Skijäger* discovering what fighting in open spaces was like. But the outflanking maneuver by the Russians to the north and farther south, aimed at the industrial regions of Upper Silesia onto which the 17. Armee was backing, was getting more pronounced, gradually reducing the width of the corridor, and the opportunity for 1.SJD and the rest of the army, threatened on all sides, to fall back west.

The commanding officer of the army group, Field Marshal Schörner, agreed to a withdrawal during the night of January 27/28. The retreat began on February 8 with 8.PzD but the Russians didn't miss it, as they were trying to drive a wedge between 1.SJD and 97.JgD. Particularly intense hand-to-hand fighting took place in the sector. However, Soviet pressure diminished progressively from mid-February onward, a partial respite for the units that were starting to run out of ammunition, especially the artillery.

On February 16/17, 97.JgD deployed back south of Racibórz, to the banks of the Oder. A reinforced GJR91 (4.GD) joined 68.ID between Racibórz and Rybnik. Anticipating a planned attack for March 10 (a Soviet POW had talked), and rather than see its positions crushed by Soviet artillery, Stalin's organs (Katyushas), and the Red Air Force, OB 17. Armee launched an attack during the night of the 8th/9th to the north of Racibórz.

The surprise didn't last long, and very soon Soviet artillery as well as armored counterattacks caused enormous losses among the *Skijäger*. Then, on March 15, the Red Army launched their big offensive on the northern flank of Upper Silesia, on the Neisse, around Glatz with the usual scenario: artillery bombardment and Stalin's organs, fighter-bombers, and massed armor and infantry.

Facing 1.SJD, 97.JgD, and their neighboring units, the enemy broke through at Cosel, to the north of Racibórz on March 16, advancing west. 371.ID and 18.SS-Panzergrenadier-Division Horst Wessel were knocked about. Elements from 1.SJD assigned to 371.ID were destroyed, including III./SJR2, completely, but it was quickly reconstituted.

The linkup of Soviet forces that had broken through farther south was foreseen for the 18th, with the encirclement of LVI.AK (Korpsgruppe Schlesien, Lieutenant General Koch-Erpach). The situation rapidly degenerated into chaos, with localized units attacking and counterattacking in all directions for 12 days, with heavy losses on both sides.

In the night of March 31/April 1,1945, what was left of the units broke off and positioned themselves at Troppau and in the neighboring countryside, 20 kilometers to the south of Racibórz, where they enjoyed a few days of relative calm. On April 15, the Soviets launched a powerful attack with six divisions against 1.SJD at Troppau and, on both sides of the road from Racibórz. The *Skijäger* repelled the assault as well as an attempt to outflank them by the east the next day. In the days that followed, part of I./SJR1 established its defenses on old Czech fortifications. Losses were mounting and the *Skijäger* of *Festung Troppau* earned the moniker *Gräberfeld* (graveyard) for Fortress Troppau. By April 22, there were only 23 *Jäger* left in fighting condition in I./SJR1.

On the 25th, the Russians succeeded in knocking out 1.SJD's defenses, whose remnants were falling back a few kilometers to the west and south of Troppau, now abandoned to the enemy. But the Soviets did not continue their operation against 1.SJD's new sector: they veered off west toward Mährich-Ostrau (today Ostrava, in the Czech Republic), a big steel town in the heart of a mining region. As the divisional commander, General Hundt, was dead, no doubt killed in combat, Colonel Weiler, commander of SJR1, took over from him (he committed suicide on May 8).

The death of the Führer was officially announced on May 1. The same day, and also on the 3rd, 1.SJD attacked north alongside 16.PzD and the Führer-Begleitdivision around Troppau. On May 6, Grand-Admiral Dönitz, the new head of the German government, ordered all units to save as many troops as possible and fall back west in utmost haste.

During the night of May 7/8, the division received an order from XXXX.PzK to continue to Landskron, to position itself there as a barrage. On May 8, 1945, the division set off westward, toward the Moldau, staying grouped together as long as possible, the

The 8.8cm PaK 43 was the ultimate version of the wheeled antitank weapon, painted yellow when it came out of the factory, then white. The size of the *Gebirgsjäger* gives an idea of the gun's height. (DR)

This particularly striking trench scene is by Franz Eichorst, entitled "*Kampfpause*" (a break in the fighting), on view in the United States.

rear covered by the Ski-Füsilier-Bataillon. But after a few kilometers, the routes were quickly blocked by the Soviets and several groups tried to exfiltrate through the woods. (One German tank commander in a captured T-34 from 4./Schweres-Ski-Bataillon (SSB) tried to slip into a Soviet column advancing west but his machine broke down.) Few succeeded and the *Skijäger* were marched off into captivity.

Army Groups North Ukraine and South Ukraine, Summer 1944–Spring 1945

The Red Army reached 3.GD (under Major General Paul Klatt since July, having an unhealthy turnover of commanders) positions in the Draceni sector in August 1944. Indeed, on August 20, in the aftermath of *Bagration*, the Russians facing Army Group Center launched their operation toward Jassy and Kichinev (Chişinău), which led to 6. Armee being annihilated. And, in Romania, following the August 23 putsch which toppled Marshal Antonescu's pro-German government, Romanian units quickly turned against their former German allies.

3. and 4.GDen were obliged to abandon their positions, notably 3.GD at Draceni on August 25. The Soviets then engaged the Germans in the northern Carpathians, with 3.GD in the Bistritz Valley which it abandoned on September 7, outflanked on its southern side by the Soviets, and fell back to the Mures sector. There the division destroyed two Soviet regiments between September 24–30, 1944. From October 8, with the pressure of the operational situation and anticipating the Führer's authorization on the 17th, 3.GD started to fall back toward Transylvania (Siebenbürgen) where heavy fighting broke out in the Satu Mare sector on October 21.

That same evening, 3.GD crossed into Hungary and hurried to Nyiregyhaza, north of Debrecen, which the Soviets had occupied on the 22nd. In position on the 24th, 3.GD with 23.PzD attacked northwestward, driving against the flanks of three Soviet army corps, on October 26.

Cases of collective rape of Hungarian women by the Soviets were identified and used by the German command to prepare its own nationals for the same fate. Beyond Hungary lay a faithful German ally, the *Ostmark* (Austria), and therefore Reich territory.

At the beginning of November 1944, 3.GD crossed over to the west bank of the Tisza (Theiss)—to the southeast of the town of Miskolc that specialized in the armaments industry—clinging onto two bridgeheads to the east of the river. Workers from the Hungarian arsenals revolted against the Germans and GJR144 was obliged to engage them. The division fought in the Miskolc region, with heavy losses, then across the Bükk range in the north of Hungary, and finally, after a brief rest, at Putnok, in December 1944.

Faced with the strength of the Red Army thrust aimed at encircling Budapest, 3.GD, like its neighbors, suffered heavy losses and was ordered to retreat toward Sajo and Rimava in Slovakia, on the northern sides of the Beskides, then to the south of Schwarzwasser (Čierna Voda), toward Saybusch on the banks of the Vistula, then again to Schwarzwasser.

The Soviets caught up with the German division, and heavy fighting, often hand to hand, ensued between December 10–25. Finally, in January 1945, the situation stabilized along the passes in the Upper Tatras (Sillein/Žilina and Jablunka) in Slovakia, the division finding itself confronted with Slovak partisans supported by the Soviets.

On the 29th, GJR138 suffered heavy losses due to the partisans. At the end of January, the division was once again confronted with the Soviets and a division of Romanian cavalry. On February 10, 3.GD continued falling back to the west across the center of Slovakia and the Tatra Mountains, in the region where in 1939 it had been deployed to invade Poland. It then joined XXXXIX.Geb.-AK under Lieutenant General Karl von Le Suire (since August 5); because of changes in the reporting structure, it was afforded a complete GJR. When the Red Army took Bratislava, the division crossed over to the west of the Vistula, in the Kattowitz sector.

In the Bratislava (Pressburg) region, the Osttürkischer Waffenverband der SS was involved in limited fighting against Slovak partisans from January to the end of March 1945. Ultimately, with the Red Army closing in, the unit switched to northern Italy (see the later chapter "Italy, 1943–45").

From March 10–15, a Soviet breakthrough obliged 3.GD to commit a whole battery of Sturmgeschützen from Geb.-P.J.A.95. It continued to withdraw, this time north and toward Upper Silesia, in the Troppau and Olmutz regions, alongside 4.GD, also in the same corps (see Army Group Center above). Pushed westward by the Soviets, this division from XXXXIX.Geb.-AK finished the war in Bohemia-Moravia in the Olmutz–Brodek region, where it surrendered on May 8, 1945. Few managed to reach the American lines.

Skijäger from the Skijäger-Brigade in their characteristic fall turnout: reversible white and green Windbluse and Windhose, canvas equipment painted white for a Maschinepistole MP 43 (called the "Sturmgewehr" which coined the term "assault rifle" which is still used today), weapons painted white, painted canvas and leather mittens (the motorcyclist's model), and Skischuhe (ski boots). White Bergmütze covers, or caps painted white, camouflage masks, and overboots, were only distributed in winter as extras, with the skis. (DR)

Norway and Finland, 1942–45

In early December 1942, fearing an Allied landing between Drontheim and Narvik, in coordination with a Soviet offensive, AOK Norwegen asked for reinforcements, including a Polizei regiment, having in mind 28. Jäger-Division. Securing the army's rear was in fact entrusted to a Luftwaffe infantry division and a Polizei regiment—Polizei-Gebirgsjäger-Regiment 18 (renamed SS-Polizei-Gebirgsjäger-Regiment 18 in February 1943 in accordance with a directive (*Verfügung*) from *Reichsführer-SS und Chef der Deutschen Polizei* Heinrich Himmler)—that comprised three battalions of Schutzpolizei with solid experience in anti-partisan operations in mountainous and snowbound regions, which had arrived in Finland later that month.

Tactically subordinated to "Nord" (6. SS-Gebirgs-Division Nord) for three months, in the rear of *Abschnitt* (Sector) Louhi, the unit got accustomed to this new theater of operations which was in sharp contrast to summer in Slovenia (see the later chapter "The Balkans, 1942–45").

The regiment moved up to the front at the end of January, continuing its material preparation (transporting an artillery group and an antitank company requested by the Ordnunsgpolizei) and remained in Karelia until the end of July. Indeed, on June 21, at

Distributing ammunition was done from clearly identified points, equipped with a telephone (indicated by a white lightning flash on a red background) after being delivered by boat-sledges (*Akjas*). The *Jäger* wear sheepskin coats; they have empty rucksacks to draw issues for other soldiers. (Ehrt Archives)

Sledges were part of the equipment issued at all levels.

This casualty is being evacuated on a makeshift stretcher, in a thick fur blanket, still indispensable in early spring. This could be a realistic training session, since some of the men are wearing reversed fatigue jackets, usually reserved for the bivouac, or base camps. (Ehrt Archives)

After Demelhuber, who was responsible for establishing the unit, General Matthias Kleinheisterkamp, the second commander of the "Nord," took over at the beginning of 1942. He is welcomed here by *SS-Standartenführer* (Colonel) Dr Wilhelm Petersen, the division's Senior Medical Officer. (DR)

The Karelia Front was established as a secondary front at the end of the summer of 1941. This *Gulaschkanone* (field kitchen) is out of sight and out of the direct line of fire.

the request of the Reichsführer, the regiment was withdrawn from AOK 20.Geb.A to fight partisans in the southeastern theater. It was therefore transported by sea to Danzig then to Greece, arriving in mid-August. The artillery group only caught up with it in Greece.

Preparation began in June with patrols to locate precise objectives. On June 8, Operation *Emil*, Emil being the first name of Colonel Schuler, commander of GJR218, was launched. The objective was to take a fortified crest, the *Bunkerrücken*, one kilometer from *HKL*, along a two-kilometer front, facing its southern positions. These heights were an excellent observation platform for the Russians: they had constructed defensive strongpoints made of logs.

"Nord" organized a deception operation—a dummy regimental attack. The assault by a reinforced GJR218, preceded by a heavy artillery barrage (GAR82 reinforced by a battery of recoilless howitzers and a battalion from "Nord") and PaKs firing at bunkers, was launched at midday. Taking the perfectly camouflaged backup positions, starting with the Sukkula point to the north of the crest, lasted the whole day, using explosives and flamethrowers in hand-to-hand fighting, despite energetic attention from enemy *Jabos*. The seriously wounded were evacuated by foot then by seaplane from Lake Top.

On 10th, then again on the 13th, 14th, 18th, and finally the 22nd, the Soviets tried to take back the heights, employing massive artillery and Katyusha barrages, air attacks (using, among others,

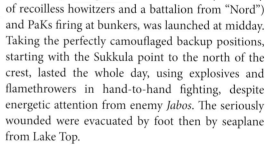

The Liza became the "river of destiny" for the Gebirgskorps Norwegen. In temperatures of -49°F, positions had to be held by well-wrapped-up *Gebirgsjäger*, prepared at all times for Soviet attacks. This propaganda postcard by F. Trenk is of an MG-Schütze 1.

Recreation of uniform ensemble from the "Nord" division during the summer of 1942 using period items. The *Feldbluse* (field blouse) M40 insignia were the classic SS runes and the left-hand *Kragenspiegel* (collar patch) of an *SS-Mann*, a simple soldier; the *Schulterklappe* is black, lined with *Feldgrau* and with artillery-red piping. The *Bergmütze* were introduced gradually in the winter of 1941/2. In certain cases, they were Wehrmacht Heer models with Waffen-SS insignia. The edelweiss on the arm and on the *Bergmütze* only appeared in October 1943. The "Nord" cuff band was only worn in the two *GJRs* until the regimental bands seen later appeared; it was introduced in the command and support arms toward the end of 1941 and retained until the end. (Private collections)

phosphorus bombs) and flamethrowers. The *"VB"* (*vorgeschobene Beobachter*, or forward artillery observers), even though they'd been bypassed, directed supporting fire onto their own positions. Sappers, radio operators, medics, and messengers took up arms. Neither the *Bunkerrücken* nor Sukkula fell to the enemy, who lost a thousand men and around 50 bunkers. The terrain was completely ploughed up and trees smashed. The crest was renamed *Schulerrücken*. A cable winch was set up to the summit by AOK20.

In September, powerful Soviet elements tried to take 6.GD's positions, in *Abschnitt* Murmansk, especially those of GJR141, backed onto the Titovka. Major General Ritter von Hengl had just taken over as divisional head from Schörner who had been transferred to the southern sector of the Eastern Front.

The beginning of 1944 was relatively calm for 20.Geb.A. units. Its mountain divisions (2., 6. and 7.GDen, Div.-Gruppe Kräutler, and 6.SS Nord, as well as skier units from XXXVI. AK under Vogel) held the northern tip of the German positions which were mainly static, where manning observation positions, patrolling and undertaking logistics tasks like the maintenance of communication lines or portage alternated with each other. In early February 1944, the German high command ordered AOK20 to take over the Uchtua sector, to the south of *Abschnitt* Louhi, in order to relieve Finnish units which went into the reserve.

Delivery of supplies to the Finns was assured by the Germans who, in spite of their hesitance in considering that their ally might change sides, wanted to demonstrate how solid the alliance was. The high command was concerned about the strategic aspect of maintaining 20.Geb.-Armee in place: controlling Finnish nickel (98 percent of the European resources), as with Swedish iron ore at Narvik, was indispensable for continuing the war. Ominously, there were, however, intense negotiations during the first six months of 1944 between the Finnish and Soviet governments, with Sweden's intercession. This separate peace the Russians were proposing was proving difficult for the Finns to accept. The period of thaw was not favorable for a major attack, all the more so that, according to the Germans, the Russians seemed to want to spare the Finnish forces and only attack the 20.Geb.-Armee.

In March 1944, 7.GD began taking over this new sector—where it relieved the Finnish 14th Infantry Division—and in April transferred the *HKL* to Div.-Gruppe Kräutler. Once the snow had thawed, the division was given the task of getting the roads and fortified positions back into condition, in totally different circumstances, rubber boots often replacing the *Bergschuhen*. The Soviets very quickly started harassing these positions: raids, phosphorus and snipers being tactics of choice.

From March onward, Soviet units were detected moving up into the line facing AOK20, in particular in front of the Kandalaksha sector. On April 27, the Soviets bombarded the positions on the Liza for three days, but only attacked in mid-May, and at company level. From June 10–18, they attacked Finnish troops in the Viipuri (Viborg) region in an effort to at least neutralize them.

This bloodletting was decisive in regard to what followed. The German command had Panzerfausten brought in by fast launch and then 5,000 Panzerschrecke by air at the end of June. But the Soviets' intention was clear: by hitting a key zone and targeting specific units, they maintained enormous operational pressure in support of the diplomatic negotiations, this military crisis triggering a political crisis. The first Finnish units incorporated into the German defensive sectors were withdrawn, in spite of the fact that the Finnish government— which the Socio-Democrats had just quit—was aware of the opening of the Normandy Front

The numerous pauses in the fighting allowed training activities to continue for replacement personnel. (Ehrt Archives)

A *Jagdkommando* from "Nord" posing after its return from a patrol. (Colorized document. DR)

and the launch of *Bagration* (see earlier chapter "The Eastern Front, 1942–45") along the entire Eastern Front on the 23rd.

Colonel General Dietl crashed aboard his Junkers Ju 52 in the Semmering on June 23, 1944. The day before he'd had a particularly stormy meeting with Hitler, in which he had expressed strong opinions about the pursuit of the war. (Dietl was pleading for Northern Europe and Crete to be abandoned in favor of concentrating on defending the Reich against the East. Some historians consider his death as "mysterious.") Lieutenant General Karl Eglseer, the general commanding XVIII.Geb.-AK, was killed with him. The Austrian, Colonel General Lothar Rendulic, was Dietl's immediate successor, followed by *General der Gebirgsjäger* Böhme in January 1945. Lieutenant General Hohbaum took command of XVIII.Geb.-AK.

The Soviets tried to outmaneuver XVIII.Geb.-AK on June 29, 1944 and attacked positions to the north of Lake Ssenosero. Ski-Btl.82—assigned to "Nord" by 7.GD when it changed sector in the spring—and the division's motorized battalion (SS-Schützen-Btl.6) constituting Kampfgruppe Lapp, tried to block the breakthrough. The fighting took place from July 1–18; GJR139, and Ski-Btle.83 and 367 also took part.

Soviet artillery and raids were particularly destructive. Evacuating the wounded via boat was impossible. Medics had to set up field hospitals so they could perform serious operations before the *Sturmboote* were at last able to arrive and evacuate the critically wounded.

The Soviet command seemed to consider these operations as crucial: they were often carried out by units consisting of only officers and political commissars. At the same time, Colonel Schuler had his officers reconnoiter a position they could fall back on near the Swedish frontier to the northwest of Karesuando, the *Sturmbock-Stellung* (Battering Ram Line) to prevent a Finnish attack toward the Lyngenfjord which, in line with Tromsø, could cut off the units retreating through the Great North. This action would contribute to the German delaying maneuver in October.

The End of the German Presence in Finland and Norway

Rendulic's first decision, as early as June, considering how the whole of the Eastern Front and the situation in Finland was evolving generally, was to start planning Operation *Birke* (*Birch*) and Operation *Nordlicht* (*Northern Lights*, not to be confused with the September 1942 operation in Leningrad)—evacuating Finland and withdrawing 20.Geb.-Armee into Norway.[1] Three major routes were available: to the north by Petsamo and Kirkenes, then along the Barents Sea (the opposite route to that used in 1941); the favorite, in the center between Minio and Lyngen; and to the south by Rovaniemi, the Gulf of Bothnia, and the

---

1 A third operation, Operation *Tanne* (Operation *Fir Tree*), was intended to capture the islands in the Gulf of Bothnia but no mountain units were available.

The transport of supplies very soon created almost insoluble problems for the AOK Norwegen command, who were forced to adopt methods like those deployed in mountainous regions. This series of photographs shows a simplified logistics chain, a succession of methods used, depending on the terrain (very few roads) and the operations in progress: the lorry (here from 2.GD displaying its tactical markings, the reindeer's head), the heavy horse-drawn trailer (*schwere Heeresfeldwagen* or *Hf.2*), then the light two-wheeled (*leichter Heeresfeldwagen* or *Hf.1*) trailer; the porter companies (*Gebirgsträger*) which could be translated as "mule companies," used mules, Haflingers or regional horses, or men's backs mounted with regulation wooden external frame backpacks with leather suspenders (*Tragekarren*). Fresh or processed supplies were then distributed to porters from the front who would then deliver them in turn to their comrades on the frontlines. The Gebirgs-Träger-Btle 55, 56, and 57 had been levied in August 1939 and were engaged in Norway and Finland until 1945, respectively as organic units of XIX.Geb.-AK, XXXVI.Geb.-AK, and AOK20. Gebirgs-Träger-Btl 56 became Heeres-Gebirgsträger-Btl Allgäu on January 28, 1945 in Norway. Gebirgs-Träger-Btle 67 and 68, both levied in August 1939 for respectively 2. and 3.GDen, were disbanded at the beginning of 1940. These units were all recruited in Germany. (Ehrt Archives)

Baltic. *Birke* did not exclude a passive response from the Finns; *Nordlicht*, a follow-on operation from *Birke* in the summer, envisaged a retreat in force. Among the measures was establishing fortified sectors, the *Sturmbock-Stellung* (see above) as well as the *Ivalo-Stellung* in the rear of 20.Geb.-Armee—at the start of an important route north, at the entrance of the corridor to the Lyngenfjord.

Taking Narva enabled the Russians to enter Latvia and drive a wedge between the Finnish forces and the Germans in the south. The collapse of Army Group Center during Operation *Bagration* would only destabilize Germany's allies, who deserted one by one. On August 4, Mannerheim was sworn in and became the President of the Finnish Republic. On the 5th, the Soviets resumed their attack against the Mannerheim Line in East Karelia, but were driven off by the Finns.

On September 2, 1944, Finland announced that it was putting an end to its relations with Germany and that it was starting peace talks with the USSR. The government allowed the German forces until September 15 to leave the country on pain of internment. It changed sides on the same day by declaring war on Germany … but only formally announced this at the beginning of March 1945. The new Paasiviki government, which the Communists had joined after the fighting had ended, wanted to formalize the situation to provide guarantees to the Soviets so they would not occupy the country. Nevertheless, the first Finno-German confrontations would force the Germans to leave the country.

What was at stake for XIX.Geb.-AK (Lieutenant General Ferdinand Jodl) with its 2. (under Major General Hans Degen) and 6.GD (Major General Max-Josef Pemsel, Major General Remold after April 1945), up until then engaged in the far north of Karelia, was covering the withdrawal of the other two army corps of 20.Geb.-Armee engaged in the center of Finland which in fact had to fall back by the north behind XIX.Geb.-AK.

They were facing Soviet forces that would immediately take advantage of this turnaround in the alliance and attack in force from Murmansk. *Abschnitt* Louhi (7.GD, now centered on Uchtua, Div.-Gruppe Kräutler, and "Nord") started pulling out during the night of September 7/8 (following order *Birke Anschlag*, or "Cutting down the Birches"), covered toward the southeast by motorized elements, like M.G.-Ski-Brigade Finnland, Geb.-A.A.99, and Geb.-PzJg-Abt 99 from 7.GD. *Abschnitt* Kandalakscha started pulling out during the evening of September 10. Finnish forces landing in the first week of October at Tornio which blocked the retreat of German forces by the ports on the Gulf of Bothnia—which lasted until September 20—constituted a *casus belli*.

On October 5, Rendulic triggered *Nordlicht*, the withdrawal in force. The Finns were hot on the heels of the XIX.Geb.-AK rearguard. They were partly equipped with German-issued weapons (Panzerfaust, Panzerschreck, Sturmgeschütze) and used the *Motti* (*Kessel* in German, or cauldron) tactic of isolating enemy pockets, encircling them then destroying them. After securing Pudasjärvi at the end of September, the corps held a recovery line between Kemi (Gulf of Bothnia) and Ylimaa–Posio, 60 kilometers to the south of Rovaniemi. The aim was to enable HQs, services, and depots for the entire AOK20 to be evacuated. The defensive positions were basic, the fall weather having already inundated the marshes. The first snows fell in early October.

Div.-Gruppe Kräutler and "Nord" had also managed their withdrawal and found themselves to the west of 7.GD between Kemi and Tornio, on the Swedish border, at the

The Regiment Hofmeister, whose name is displayed above the entrance of this comfortable-looking building, was GJR136 from 2.GD, and not Kampfgruppe Hoffmeister which had reached the Finnish front at the end of July, after a break in the Army Group North sector, in the Staraia Russia sector. The guard on duty is wearing a machine gunner's *Mantel*, with leather shoulder pads. (Ehrt Archives)

With the coming of winter 1942/3, frontline positions were consolidated and improved upon all the time.

The daily fare was improved by local resources, notably superb wild pike "which Ivan won't have!" The cold has come with the first snows and the *Windjacke* has reappeared. The almost troglodyte-style of living quarters is rather elaborate, a constant feature of the German policy of preserving combat strength. (Ehrt Archives)

51

Jäger patrolling lines of barbed wire, looking for traces of enemy infiltration along the coast. (DR)

top of the Gulf of Bothnia. Div.-Gruppe K., reinforced by MG.-Ski-Brigade and II/GJR206 (soon to be annihilated), was engaged in retaking Tornio, taken by two divisions of Finnish infantry disembarked at the top end of the Gulf of Bothnia. It then fell back northward on October 8 along the Kemijoki Valley. On the 15th, it joined 7.GD in the same sector, having abandoned vehicles and carts, sometimes with their packs.

During the night of October 6/7, the final elements of XVIII.Geb.-AK were recovered around Ylimaa. The Finns approached GJR218's positions, a sketch of its installations having fallen into their hands. The fighting was difficult to coordinate, as the Finns were natural fighters with an innate sense of territory, vanishing after an attempt at encirclement, and only re-emerging a few hours later in the same spot, or infiltrating the German positions in small groups which made their intentions unclear.

German reinforcements, on an ad hoc basis in the form of tanks, included some T-34s. Heavier snowfalls transformed the routes into traps, at times with the mules sinking and disappearing into the marshes. Winter equipment had not as yet been issued and the warmest item was the overcoat. After three days' intense fighting, the Germans fell back from Ylimaa to a new defensive line around Taipale, 30 kilometers east of Rovaniemi. The Finns, after relieving their lead elements who had suffered significant losses, resumed the chase and made contact on the 13th with the reinforced GJR218, at Taipale.

That same evening, this regiment broke off and reached Rovaniemi, but had to return during the night to extricate Geb.-A.A.99 encircled in a *Motti*, and who risked capture and handover to the Russians. The return, a challenge for the regimental commander Colonel Schüler, ended in brutal hand-to-hand fighting but enabled a maximum of *Jäger* and scouts to reach the German lines. Schüler was awarded the Knight's Cross for his actions. The two reinforcement companies from "Nord" reached Rovaniemi via Tornio and were immediately committed to the battle, contributing to the successful outcome.

Div.-Gruppe Kräutler, 7.GD, MG-Ski-Brigade, and other elements moved north along two routes, the westernmost hugging the Swedish border. "Nord" took up the rearguard after Rovaniemi was abandoned on October 16 in ruins.

The difficulties of maneuvering a 7.5cm M36 mountain gun in thick snow, with hidden hollows. (DR)

The 3.7cm PaK gun positions in this unit are linked by radio, making for easier command and control. The gun servers are wearing one-piece overalls. The shelter is made of logs and covered with snow. (DR)

A field hospital has been set up behind 2.GD's positions utilizing barracks and tents. The vehicles are German but also with some captured British. (Ehrt Archives)

At the end of December 1942, Polizei-Gebirgsjäger-Regiment 18, ski and mountain specialists, was welcomed by "Nord," having incorporated three battalions already deployed. Colonel Frantz, the commanding officer, poses with his officers. The basic uniform is that of the Schutzpolizei, initially with brown cuffs, then wholly *Grünmeliert* (dyed blue-green) with light green distinctives close to the color of the *Jäger* arm with an edelweiss on the bottom of the left-hand sleeve. Some men also wore a *Deutsche Wehrmacht* black cuff title on the same arm, showing they were a combat unit. The guard on the left is wearing the first model Waffen-SS parka, the *Charkov*. (Poys Archives)

Distinctive insignia of the Norwegian skier battalion, the only unit with foreign recruits within AOK20 Norwegen: the nationality escutcheon in Norwegian colors and BEVo cuff title. (Private collections)

Ski-Bataillon Norge

A single mountain unit with foreign recruits was formed under command of 20.Gebirgs-Armee, the SS-Skijäger-Bataillon Norge. During the summer of 1942, a Danish Waffen-SS volunteer, married to a Norwegian, a teacher of physics and head of a Norwegian National Socialist youth movement, Gust Jonassen, suggested to Waffen-SS officers that they form a unit of SS skiers made up of Norwegian volunteers.

The idea was approved by the command and recruitment began, initially using skiing capabilities as a criterion. Those who had been trained as officers were selected for the command posts. In September 1942, the company was sent for initial training to the center at Cernay (Sennheim) in Alsace, and the future officers to the officer school (*SS-Junkerschule*) at Bad Tölz, in Bavaria. The infantry training—wearing paratroopers' helmets—lasted until Christmas after which the ski company was assembled for ski training at a police training camp near Dresden with Polizei instructors, the only ones available to the Waffen-SS. However, there was no snow in the region.

The soldiers joined their officers and NCOs, some of whom were German, near Danzig in early February 1943. The unit's creator, *SS-Obersturmführer* (First Lieutenant) Gust Jonassen, took command on May 26, 1943.

The unit reached the front where it was subordinated to SS-Aufkl.-Abt. 6 "Nord" until July, enduring its baptism of fire while skirmishing. In September 1943, it was decided to increase the unit to battalion size. Apart from new recruits, personnel were taken from PzGren-Rgt 23 Norge so as to create a tactical pawn that was entirely Norwegian, with the designation SS-Skijäger-Bataillon Norge (SJB N).

This new unit, consisting of a *Stabskompanie* with three companies of skiers, was assembled at the military camp at Oulu, behind Nord's operational area. The officers, youngsters for the most part, had obtained solid experience in the Freiwilligen-Legion Norwegen, part of the Wiking Division.

In January, the battalion was engaged on the northern flank of "Nord," in the hilly region of Kaprolat toward Lake Tiksje, in the northeast of Finland. Apart from holding fortified positions, it patrolled all sectors looking for traces of Soviet incursions along the front which had been virtually static since the end of 1941. At the end of March 1944, the battalion came into contact with the Soviets and fighting ensued with heavy losses on both sides.

For the record, another unit of Norwegian recruits was engaged in "Nord:" 2.Polizei-Kompanie. It was equipped entirely as a Waffen-SS unit but without any ski or mountain specialty. It was merged temporarily with 1./SJB Norge which had been all but annihilated in March. It was only in April 1944 that a Norwegian, *SS-Hauptsturmführer* (Captain) Frode Halle, took over the battalion, commanded until then by a German.

A recruitment poster for Ski-Bataillon Norge with the unit's name in Norwegian.

This white *Windbluse* was similar in cut to that for the Wehrmacht-Heer which appeared in 1942, but was not reversible and had no strap passing between the legs; it was issued to "Nord," at least to the skiers. (Private collection)

On June 25, the Russians launched a significant attack against the Kaprolat Hills, and encircled SJB Norge which was only just disengaged on the 26th by the Reinhard Heydrich Regiment.

The rest of the summer was taken up reinforcing positions along the Sohjana River. By September, the battalion had been re-formed with 200 young recruits as reinforcements. But then Finland changed sides, precipitating the German withdrawal which SJB Norge took part in covering. Thus, on the evening of October 16, alongside the Michael Gaißmair Regiment, it counterattacked, assaulting the Finnish forces pursuing them through the forests north of Rovaniemi. A few skirmishes marked the withdrawal to the Norwegian border. Once back in Norway, the unit was absorbed into the police and became the SS-Polizei-Grenadier-Bataillon (mot.) 506.

There had been intense Soviet reconnaissance activity at the beginning of October 1944 in front of XIX.Geb.-AK, the deployment of air force units near the front, as well as increasingly intense artillery duels. A major Soviet offensive was in the offing, aimed at the army corps protecting 20.Geb.-Armee's withdrawal toward Norway along the Barents Sea, and the link between Petsamo and Kirkenes. On October 7, after a two-and-a-half-hour artillery bombardment, the 7th and 14th Soviet Armies of the Karelia Front, a total of six army corps, launched a massive attack against the northern sector of AOK20's front—from north to south, 6.GD, 2.GD, and 163.ID—employing different tactics than had been used before. The Soviets took advantage of the fragility of the German defensive system: the 6–10-kilometer intervals between strongpoints in some sectors and particularly XVIII.AK and XXXVI.AK units withdrawing and destabilizing the rear by jamming the few existing roads. The Soviets managed to infiltrate large numbers of infantry, quickly reinforced by armored units, which soon overran the German positions. 6.GD was forced to abandon its initial defensive positions on the heights of the Liza, then those of the Titovka, while 2.GD retreated to its second line of defense.

At the same time, Soviet amphibious units (12th Navy Infantry Division) following the 14th Army, landed on the coast at Motowski Bay. On the 9th, two Soviet regiments, preceding the two army corps, made for the *Russenstraße*—the "Russian road" that linked the Titovka to the lower source of the Liza. XIX.Geb.-AK's and 6.GD's HQs had been installed here—to

Patrolling on skis was part of the daily routine for the units in Karelia, here in the *Abschnitt* Murmansk.

These *Jäger* from "Nord" are taking advantage of more clement weather outside their shelter (*Hütte*). One of them is still wearing stone gray trousers from SS-VT, and the others wear straight *Feldgrau* trousers. (DR)

"*Frohe Weihnachten 1943!*" ("Happy Christmas 1943!"). This collection of souvenirs from the *Eismeer-Front,* placed on a camouflaged Waffen-SS *Zeltbahn*, is characteristic of the troops' artistic bent in this theater of operations. (Private collection)

the south where 6.GD merged with 2.GD. Simultaneously, a large battlegroup, the size of an army corps, outflanking 2.GD by the south after penetrating the positions in 163.ID's sector and dominating any movement on the tundra, broke through to the *Eismeerstraße*, that vital Rovaniemi–Petsamo logistics axis, arriving on the 10th. The main Soviet objective was Petsamo with the intermediary objective of Luostari. Two further Red Army corps were in reserve. The Soviets, oblivious of their massive casualties, took Petsamo on October 15.

This reenactment using period items illustrates the typical dress of a skier in the "Nord," and the Norge battalion in particular. The main items are a fur cap and white two-piece overalls. (Private collection)

An MG team in AA defense against Soviet fighter-bomber attacks. (DR)

A woven variant of the Reinhard Heydrich Regiment armband.

The SS-Gebirgsjäger-Regiment 11 Reinhard Heydrich bore the name of the Deputy Protector of Bohemia-Moravia since October 22, 1943. He was killed by Czech Resistance fighters on May 27, 1942. The RH cuff band was made by BEVo as was the SS-Gerbigsjäger-Regiment 12 Michael Gaißmair one. The latter was issued as of June 21, 1944 and evoked the man who had protested Catholic influence in Bavaria in the 16th century.

On the 18th, after crossing the Petsamo-Yoki River, both Soviet armies resumed their westward offensive. On the 19th, Nikel fell into Soviet hands as did the mines at Kolosjoki, destroyed before being abandoned. Being so close to the Norwegian border, AOK20 considered Kolosjoki—apart from its strategic and economic value—a critical defensive linchpin. If it was lost it would endanger the withdrawal to Kirkenes. On October 21, Soviet aircraft bombed the town and destroyed part of the port infrastructure, significantly the water supply for ships' boilers.

On October 22, Rendulic ordered a general withdrawal westward. On the 27th, he was appointed OB 20.Geb.-Armee and at the same time Befehlshaber Norwegen—after the Finland and Norway command was reorganized.

Intense fighting broke out around Kirkenes between October 23–25. The Germans destroyed all the infrastructure, especially the bridges. Then, at the beginning of November, leaving behind delaying elements from 7.GD and Geb.-Brigade Generaloberst Dietl, on Karesuando (*Sturmbock-Stellung*) and in the Kilpisjärvi region (*Semmering-Stellung*), the German forces began a forced march westward, along Route 50, the only proper road. As soon as the Germans crossed the border on the 22nd, the Norwegian Resistance began assisting the Soviets—hailed as liberators—while the Royal Navy Fleet Air Arm harassed the withdrawing German columns.

This *Gefreiter*, on observation among the rocks in the northern sector, is wearing a 1943/44 make of *Feldbluse* 42. (Ehrt Archives)

To cover the withdrawal of 20.Gebirgs-Armee, the *Gebirgsjäger* used the know-how acquired after more than three years in the Karelia theater.

General Dietl was killed in an air accident on June 23, 1944. Colonel General Lothar Rendulic (above), a former Austro-Hungarian officer, of Croatian origin, succeeded him with immediate effect. (DR)

The Germans had been ordered to respect all Finnish property except for buildings and bridges of operational worth. On October 28, however, Alfred Jodl, Chief of Staff of the Wehrmacht, ordered a scorched-earth policy to be put into effect in Norway, to the north of Lyngenfjord, with no regard for the civilian population. Alta, Hammerfest, Honingsvag, Karasjok, Kautokeino, Lakselv, Skjervoy, Storslett, and Kvaenangen were dynamited or destroyed by fire, as were depots and other facilities.

Defensive positions had been set up by the Todt Organization to the north of Narvik around Lyngenfjord, accessible from the north and the east from Finland.

20.Gebirgs-Armee absorbed 21. Armee (Armee Norwegen) which had been disbanded, on December 18, 1944. From this date on, OB 20.Geb.-A. also became Wehrmachtsbefehlshaber Norwegen. At the beginning of January 1945, the Finns approached the *Sturmbock-Stellung* which was abandoned on the 12th. The withdrawal

In February 1945, at General Böhme's request, it was decided to create a plaque commemorating the Lapland Campaign, confirmed a few weeks before the end of the conflict. It would therefore be the last commemorative "shield'" attributed during the war and was not made before the capitulation. British General Thorpe, whose task it was to disarm the German armed forces, authorized the wearing of denazified decorations and therefore the making of these commemorative shields went ahead. They were quite basic, because of the shortage of materials; engraved or molded insignia, like these shown here can be found, as well as cold-stamped versions with or without a counter-plate. The *Verleihungsurkunde* (award diploma) systematically bears a date after July 1, 1945, the date of the first official presentations. (Private collections)

Quite logically, the Luftwaffe didn't introduce much in the way of ski or mountain equipment. Here is a private's *Bergmütze* whose flap fastens with only one button. Also issued was a white non-reversible anorak with a large chest pocket fastened by four buttons, as well as a reversed sheepskin cap. A mountain jacket (*Bergrock*) was issued sparingly, the cut very like that of the Luftwaffe *Waffenrock*, gray-blue cloth with four pockets.
(Private collection)

towards the *Semmering-Stellung*, held by 6.GD reinforced by a brigade of infantry, was followed by that toward the Lyngen region, to the *Tauern-Stellung*, on January 31.

At the end of January, GJR206 and IV./GAR82, the last rearguards, crossed the Finno-Norwegian border without problems, all German elements having passed to the south of the Lyngenfjord. 7.GD was assembled in the Narvik region at the end of February. It continued its withdrawal southward, generally on foot as soon as it started to thaw. On May 8, it reached Lillehammer, via Mosjoen, Mo-I-Rana, Steinkier, and Drontheim.

During the winter of 1944/5, in atrocious weather conditions, with very short days, amid heavy snowfalls and ice, 200,000 men and most of their supply depots were totally withdrawn and saved from capture by the Finns and the Soviets. They had fallen back in order along the Swedish border then along the Barents Sea, using almost exclusively Norway's main northern coastal road, the damaged Route 50, interrupted by deep, steep fjords.

Apart from 2.GD and 6.SS Nord which reached Germany at the end of December 1944, to be engaged in Alsace against the French and Americans, the rest of 20.Geb.-Armee continued the war in Norway until the capitulation. On May 8, Div.-Gruppe Kräutler was given the designation 9.Gebirgs-Division retroactively as of May 6. "Nord" was added so it wouldn't be confused with the other "9th" which had been created in the Semmering (see the later chapter "The Balkans, 1942–45").

Repatriating units to Germany after the capitulation was done gradually by sea then land. 7.GD was sent to France to take part in rebuilding the country.

The last commemorative "shield" created during the Third Reich was dedicated to the Lapland Campaign, the *Lappland Schild*. The design was proposed in January 1945 but the prototype was only adopted on May 1; the awards could only be made in PoW camps.

This shot illustrates a campaign practice, especially in *Abschnitt* Louhi: Heer units using Waffen-SS camouflage, in particular during *Jagdkommando* operations, to confuse Soviet intelligence officers. These uniforms were adapted to operations in the Finnish primary forest; the wrist compass was indispensable. (DR)

| Italy, 1943–45

On May 11, 1943, fighting ceased in Tunisia. On June 12, the garrison on the island of Lampedusa surrendered to the Allies who began the conquest of Europe through Italy and, de facto, opened up the second front that Stalin so desperately wanted. On July 10, the Allies launched Operation *Husky*, invading Sicily. On July 24, Mussolini was deposed and on the 27th he was arrested.

Italy's defection on September 8, 1943, even if it wasn't a great surprise to the Germans, was rapidly followed the next day by the American landing at Salerno. The Allies' next strategic objective could only be the Italian capital, with the prospect of further landings on the Mediterranean or Adriatic coasts. Some German units took part in carrying out the measures stipulated in the plan for disarming Italian troops, triggered by the codeword *Achse* (*Axe*), but predominantly outside Italy.

The German Withdrawal along the Apennines

5.GD (Ringel) was recalled from the Eastern Front where it had been fighting within Army Group North, to join LI-Geb.-AK in Italy. From December 22, 1943 onwards, it set itself up in the Apennines, firstly along the *Reinhard-Stellung* (Reinhard Line), a line of forward positions in front of the Gustav Line which went from the mouth of the Garigliano to that of the Sangro, passing through Monte Cassino and Monte Maiella.

Major General Julius "Papa" Ringel, commander 5.GD, arrived with his division from the Leningrad Front. (DR)

Because of its experience of the Eastern Front, 5.GD quickly acclimatized. (DR)

Between artillery barrages and taking advantage of clear weather in a harsh winter, these *Gebirgsjäger* attend to their equipment. Their faces are marked, by the incessant bombardments in particular, aggravated by trying weather conditions. (Ehrt Archives)

This was then the linchpin for the first battle of Monte Cassino, from Cassino to Monte Croce (the defense on Monte Cifalco, Hill 1074, and Monte Croce), dominating the Rapido in the western sector, from Selva to the eastern slopes of La Mela, and passing through Monte Mare and Monte la Mainarde. As the preparatory work for the defense resembled what he had experienced in Russia using log bunkers, Ringel secured a hundred or so pneumatic drills to make impenetrable concrete bunkers and to make the best use of the natural caves, as he had done in the Great War. This turned out to be invaluable during the Allied artillery and air force bombardments in the weeks that followed.

He sent one of his officers to offer a similar arrangement to his neighboring divisions and to the higher command. He was not listened at the time, but a few months later two *Gesteins-Bohr-Kompanien* (stone-drilling companies) from the Western Front arrived in Italy on June 15, 1944.

Two *Hochgebirgsjäger-Bataillone*, Hoch 3 and Hoch 4, were also engaged in the sector. These high-mountain *Jäger* battalions, established on November 20, 1943 using I./GJR98 from 1.GD, at the time engaged in Dalmatia, were true "front firemen" or troubleshooters, who were dispatched to all the hotspots, sometimes underemployed given their technical skills.

Soon to be fighting side by side at Monte Cassino, *Gebirgsjäger* share their skills with the *Fallschirmjäger* of 1.FJD. (DR)

Reinforcing their positions reduced to rubble by artillery, *Gebirgsjäger* wait in the hamlets and villages for Allied tank attacks, defending their positions with their Panzerfaust. (DR)

Moving a GAR85 battery up to the front.

Hoch 4, for example, in one and a half years had been subordinated to 14 different units. Hoch 3 had been posted to Landeck and Hoch 4 to Salzburg (WK XVIII) to adopt the initial structure of the high-mountain *Jäger* battalions: a *Stab* and three companies of *Jäger*, a heavy company, and an artillery battery.

5.GD, 8.PGR (from 3.PGD), and Hoch 3 (for its first operational engagement) were attacked on January 12, 1944 by elements of the Corps Expéditionnaire Français (CEF, 2e DI Marocaine and 3e DI Algérienne) which forced their way across the Rapido. Attacks and counterattacks followed around Monte Cavallo and Monte Croce until January 24. The French ended up by calling off their attack on Attina (where 5.GD had its command post), while the American offensive on the Garigliano failed. The American and British attempt to outflank the line of defense (landings at Anzio on January 22), was quickly halted and the conflict turned into a war of position, with no dents in the German defense.

The attempt to break through in the rear of Monte Cassino turned into a war of attrition with heavy loss of life on both sides, on particularly difficult terrain and in very trying weather conditions. The CEF was withdrawn from the front line to taking the initiative on the Garigliano and in the Aurunci Mountains.

Hoch 4,[1] a battlegroup hastily made up at the end of November 1943 under Major Franz Freiherr von Ruffin, had been engaged in front of the Gustav Line, on the Sangro in the Monte Amaro–Guardiagrele sector. In December, the battalion suffered heavy losses in a counterattack at Orsogna, in 65.ID's sector, then from a *Jabo* attack, and in clashes with British patrols.

In January 1944, part of Hoch 4 was withdrawn and urgently deployed by truck to the Monte Cassino sector, leaving its 1.Kp. and its artillery battery behind (which joined the battalion three months later). Its *Troß*, or baggage train, followed by road. From the outset, faced with an emergency, Hoch 4 was sent to 90.PGD's sector where it made up the spearhead (*Speerspitze*) for a counterattack aimed at retaking the summit of Monte Castellone which dominated Monte Cassino to the north.

On February 12, on orders from Lieutenant General Baade, commander 90.ID, two battalions from 200.PGR (Colonel Baron von Behr) coming in from the west and Hoch 4 from Colle Sant Angelo to the southwest via Hill 706, launched a counterattack. The artillery barrage was terrible but the creeping barrage was not in step with the advance and many Germans fell victim to their own artillery. On 13th, Baade negotiated a truce with the

---

1 Although *Hoch* is the abbreviation for *Hochgenbirgsjäger-Bataillon*, it also means "power of" in mathematics. According to this play on words Hoch 4 could therefore be designated a "unit to the power of 4."

Coordinating operations where the divisions merged was a key point in operational success. These *Gebirgsjäger* and *Fallschirmjäger* officers illustrate the principle.

American 36th Infantry Division so that each side could recover its dead.

The Germans, Hoch 4 still in the lead, succeeded in taking the Monte Castellone plateau which was left vacant for a while as it was too exposed to Allied fire, but it remained under German control. The order to evacuate the sector was only given on May 25, a week after 1.FJD was ordered to abandon Monte Cassino. Lieutenant General Ringel, the old veteran from 5.GD since its creation, handed over command of the division to Lieutenant General August Max-Günther Schrank, also a man from the "inner circle."

During the second battle of Monte Cassino, from March 15–23, 1.FJD relieved 5.GD in the Cassino sector. Hoch 4 was only partly concerned, since the Allied thrust was mainly against the village and the monastery itself. But on April 20, for the third battle, Major von Ruffin took command of a *Kampfgruppe*, including his Hoch 4 and II./GJR100 (Captain Zwickenpflug), withdrawn from 5.GD. Its mission was to cover the northern flank of 1.FJD—over five kilometers of front, from the monastery to Monte Castellone—and to ensure liaison with the neighboring division, 44.ID Hoch- und Deutschmeister.

The *Jäger* began by setting up defensive positions which proved critical during the colossal artillery bombardment which followed. With FJR3, these mountain units bore the brunt of the Polish II Corps attacks on May 11 for the fourth and final battle of Cassino, holding out until the 26th. The *Jäger* fell back in good order to *Senger-Riegel*, a line of fortified points including Panther tanks' turrets set up as casemates, manned by 2./FschPzJg-Abt.1 from 1.FJD, behind the *Gustav-Stellung* in line with Piedimonte San Germano.

In order to cover 1.FJD's withdrawal, Kampfgruppe von Ruffin positioned itself between this village and Monte Cairo (1,669 meters) with an advanced position (*Oberfähnrich*, or Senior Ensign, Keck's platoon, II./GJR100) blocking the Passo Corno and the Pizzo Corno. This subunit resisted all day on May 19 against a Polish brigade until it ran out of ammunition, thus forcing most of the battalion to reposition itself.

With the *Jabo* threat, the *Gebirgsjäger* from 5.GD always had their machine guns at the ready. (NAC)

In April/May 1944, Kampfgruppe von Ruffin ensured liaison and the continuity of the defense between 1.FJD on Monte Cassino and 44.ID Hoch- und Deutschmeister. One officer is wearing an edelweiss; he could also belong to Geb.Jg.Kp.190 of 90.PGD. (DR)

Having only received the order to fall back late during the night of 16th/17th, the *Kampfgruppe* with its *Troß*, exfiltrated north through the American lines along the Melfa Valley which had not been held open. Between February 1 and May 27, Hoch 4 and II./GJR100 lost 60 percent of their operational capacity, i.e. 828 troops.

During the night of June 4/5, 1944, Rome was declared an open city and the Allies entered the first of the European capitals to be liberated.

5.GD had held its positions from December 1943 to the beginning of May 1944 and suffered heavy losses. After being relieved by 1.FJD, 5.GD joined LI.Geb.-AK without a moment's rest, on the eastern flank of the German positions, on the Dora Line then the Albert Line. The corps waited there for the enemy, while repelling the Italian Resistance attempting to destroy logistics and telephone links.

5.GD was faced with a powerful Allied thrust—Poles and the Italian Liberation Corps (ILC)—in the Macerata sector on June 22, south of Ancona, near Perugia. On July 9, while still holding its own positions, 5.GD had to mount a counterattack into 114.JgD's weakened positions which enemy elements had managed to infiltrate.

On the 11th, 5.GD retook the sector around Pietralunga, far behind its own lines. Attacks, breakthrough attempts, and counterattacks continued for a month. Finally, a withdrawal to the Gothic Line was ordered on August 12, 1944. On the 15th, the day

the Allies landed in Provence, the planners were no longer in any doubt: the Allies would not be concentrating on the Liguria coastline but on the South of France, with a brief threat to northern Italy across the Alps.

Gen.Kdo.II.Geb.-AK was also engaged on the Italian Front but without any mountain divisions in its order of battle. After the Anzio-Nettuno landing (January 22, 1944), from January

This 8cm Nebelwerfer team demonstrates how the terrain was used as cover, especially the crevices in the rocks. (DR)

Oberjäger (Sergeant) Novak shows how exhausted the *Gebirgsjäger* were to the east of Monte Cassino. Bunkers were also made of logs like on the Leningrad Front. (Novak Archives)

On Ringel's initiative, units equipped with pneumatic drills were used to construct bunkers out of caves.

28 onward, the corps' mission was to defend the Tyrrhenian coast between Cecina and the mouth of the Tiber. It took part in 14. Armee's attack south of Rome and took steps to repulse any further landings farther north, perhaps up to the Liguria coast.

Created at the beginning of June 1944, Gebirgsjäger-Lehrbataillon Mittenwald, composed mainly of instructors and high-mountain specialists, was assigned to the Italian theater for operations on the Abruzzi (Gothic Line) on June 11. It was ordered on the 24th to deploy along the Italian Riviera to block the road from Livorno to the Apennines in case of an Allied landing in Liguria in the Livorno region. The battalion was attached to the new Army Group Ligurien whose HQ was made up of Armee-Abteilung von Zangen/Gen.Kdo. LXXXVII.AK.

Hoch 4 (at Albenga) and the Italian 4th Mountain Division (RSI) Monterosa were attached to this unit. Mittenwald reached the sector on August 24. It was then decided to create Gebirgsjäger-Regiment Meeralpen. This unit comprised a *Stab* and Hoch 4. Formed on October 26, it was an organic unit of Army Group Ligurien and was mainly engaged in the rear in the struggle against Italian partisans. It was soon assigned Geb.-Lehrbataillon Mittenwald. Hoch 3 arrived in this sector (Vintimille) in September, and was engaged on the Larche Pass alongside a battalion from GJR100. Hoch 3 was eventually rebadged III./GJR296 in 8.GD which it followed along the Gothic Line until the Armistice. (Note that although Brandenburg units were engaged during the entire Italian campaign, from Cassino to the Ligurian coast, none had the "mountain" appellation.)

German PoWs from the northern sector of Cassino at the end of the spring of 1944, captured by members of the French Expeditionary Corps. (ECPAD)

During the summer of 1944, *Geb.Panzerjäger* set up their PaK guns on roads where possible. (Polish Army Museum, NAC)

Two items of equipment (above) that were absolutely vital for 5.GD and the high-mountain *Jäger* battalions in the Cassino sector: the rucksack and the icepick (*Eispickel*). Even 1.FJD elements (right) were issued with mountain equipment better suited to their operations than their paratrooper gear, especially the *Bergschuhe* and the *Windbluse/Windhose* combinations. (Private collections)

Winter has returned to Italy, in the Abruzzi. An 8.GD artillery observer, warmly equipped after leaving the Alpine Front where he was relieved by 5.GD, sweeps the countryside of classic crests and valleys with his high-powered binoculars. (Reibert.info)

From the Gothic Line to the Po Valley

The battle for the Gothic Line—or *Grüne-Linie* (Green Line), a term preferred by Hitler—was eclipsed by the landings in Provence on August 15, 1944, with units transferred from the Allied order of battle in Italy, in particular the Corps Expéditionnaire Français and several American divisions.

The basic Allied idea was to draw the Germans toward the Adriatic coast and drive them into the center of the country toward Bologna then envelop them on the one hand, and on the other to rush north to Yugoslavia to get there before the Soviets. Planning got bogged down when winter approached the natural barrier whose operational value had been neglected: the Abruzzi.

5.GD was positioned at Romagna, to the south of Rimini and the Republic of San Marino—neutral, but occupied by 278.ID—on the right-hand wing of the corps at the end of August 1944, as part of LXXVI.PzK (*General der Panzertruppe* Traugott Herr). In front of its line of forward posts was the *Georg-Linie* (George Line), 40 kilometers in front of the Green Line against which the British V and X Corps launched a surprise attack during the night of August 25/26, with a thrust against the junction between 5.GD and its neighboring division, 71.ID. The Allies did not slow down until the Metauro (Green Line 1) which they rapidly crossed behind an artillery barrage, with a number of defensive positions unoccupied by the Germans.

5.GD, severely decimated around Cassino—some companies only had 23–30 soldiers on strength—had fallen back on Cesena-Forli, behind the Gothic Line.

Only GJR100 (Lieutenant Colonel Richard Ernst) had returned to an acceptable operational capability; it was deployed with an artillery detachment to the George Line, whereas the majority of the division was dispatched to the Alpine Front. On August 23, 1944, two battalions proceeded northwest in a vehicle convoy.

Supplies were vital, as much for the troops as for the pack animals. Cable winches—erected by the *Gebirgs-Pioniere*—which moved the hay bales were equally as important as the mules. (Sonthofen Museum)

Ullr issued several weeks before the end of the war to the *Gebirgsjäger* on the Italian Front.

The second line of defense—Green Line 2—parallel to Riccione, followed the course of the Conca. To the east, along the Adriatic coast, the Canadians—who had overtaken the Poles near the George Line—succeeded in pummeling the Germans between August 30 and September 3, so much so that Traugott Herr envisaged falling back on the *Gelbe-Stellung* (Yellow Line), level with Rimini and along the Marecchia River.

But, and this was rare in German military history, Lieutenant General Fritz Wenzel, chief of 10. Armee General Staff, overruled the instructions and ordered GJR100 to hold the village of Gemmano and the neighboring heights, and PGR71 from 29.PGD to hold the Coriano Crest, immediately to the north of Gemmano, key zones between 1.FJD and 26.PzD.

These two points, bitterly disputed in hand-to-hand fighting, cost the Allies three weeks in their thrust through to the Romagna Plain, thus leaving the Germans enough time to reorganize after this crisis period. A small village perched high up, Gemmano, and the other points on the crests (Villa, Monte Gardo, Monte Ferneto) were the scenes of bitter fighting between September 6–15, with hand-to-hand combat, and changing hands several times in a day; for GJR100, it became the "Cassino of the Adriatic." According to some, it was here that the British fought their toughest battles of the war where losses, including civilians, were heavy on both sides.

10. Armee's rearward movement toward the advanced positions of the Green Line began on August 22, 1944. LXXVI.PzK was withdrawn from the front, with 14. Armee following in a staggered sector-by-sector retreat, after August 31.

The laborers who had constructed the Green Line—the Todt Organization and Italian workers—fell back on the Po where they started working on a new line. The fighting in Apennine foothills was attritional, at least in the center of the front. Outflanked by several breakthroughs, the German command ordered a withdrawal to Green Line 2 on September 24, 1944.

On October 5, the Führer made it clear that he wanted to keep northern Italy, refusing to let his troops withdraw to the foothills of the Alps, as it would prove disastrous for German morale, as well as allowing the Allies to benefit from the agricultural riches of the Po Valley and thus being able to feed Italy's liberated zones.

By mid-October, the Allies had captured commanding positions overlooking the Po Valley. The Meeralpen Regiment was detached in November to be engaged from December 26–29 with 148.Res.Div. (LI.Geb.AK, General Valentin Feuerstein) by AOK 14 which was organizing a surprise counterattack in the Serchio Valley, in the Apuan Alps (Operation *Wintergewitter*, or *Winter Storm*). This operation, carried out in a relatively stable sector, was aimed at showing how capable the Germans were of regaining the initiative, taking prisoners and relieving the pressure on the Italian 1st Infantry Division. It achieved its objectives. A similar operation took place at the beginning of 1945; it too was successful. Meeralpen remained in the Apennines, facing the Americans and the Brazilian Expeditionary Force until the general retreat in April 1945.

Gen.Kdo.LI.Geb.-AK has been mentioned above for its part in the battle of Monte Cassino, and on the eastern flank of the Gothic Line. In January 1945, it fought without any mountain units under its command, in front of the Genghis Khan Line. It then crossed the Abruzzi, and deployed 60 kilometers from Bologna to Lake Commachio, to the right of LXXVI.PzK, then, in February, around Lake Commachio.

After the Alps, where it had taken part in heavy fighting—in particular, capturing the Vercors plateau, but more generally against the French Maquis and the Italian Resistance, and massacring French civilians—157. Reserve-Division was assigned to the Italian Front (OB Südwest) by rebadging as 8.GD (formally on February 27, 1945). It had adopted the Gebirgs-Division 44 structure on September 1. All its officers were transferred to other units following their treatment of the French civilian population. The unit was placed on standby on the Lombardy plain until December 26 when it was ordered to relieve another unit to the south of Bologna within 10 to 14 days.

On January 15, 1945 8.GD, declared operational again, was deployed to the Tagliamento, under command of XIX.PzK. It relieved 4.FJD on the 19th. Heavy snow hampered operations in this theater, limited to a few skirmishes, patrols and air activity, mainly Allied. The Brenner Pass, on the major supply route through the Alps, thus remained blocked for several weeks due to bad weather and repeated air attacks. Fighting started again with the thaw in early March 1945 with Field Marshal Kesselring's army being reinforced with a hodge-podge of contingents of differing nationalities.

The Osttürkischer Waffenverband der SS from Slovakia was engaged in the German rear, in the Merate region, 20 kilometers north of Milan at the end of March. But it would seem that it did not take part in any important operations.

Operation *Grapeshot*, a major Allied offensive, opened on April 9. 8.GD was confronted with the 6th South African Armored Division on April 14 in the Monte Sole sector, then with the US 85th and 88th Infantry Divisions in a region infested with aggressive partisans. After heavy fighting west of Bologna, in particular on April 20, the remnants of 8.GD surrendered to the Americans to the north of Verona at Rovereto, in the Trentino, on May 4.

The front collapsed on April 21 and the Germans fell back on the unprepared *Alpenvorland-Stellung* (Alps Foothills Line) in relative disorder. By April 27, the Americans had established bridgeheads north of the Po and by the following day all the German units had crossed the river. 8.GD found itself confronted by the US 10th Mountain Division around Lake Garda between the April 27 and May 1.

Fighting was to cease on May 2, 1945 in Italy; however, fighting continued until May 9, particularly to protect German soldiers from the partisans. In his history of 5.GD, *Hurra die Gams*, "Papa" Ringel, with his wide experience of the Great War in the Austro-Hungarian Army, analyzed the reasons why, according to him, the Germans could have resisted indefinitely in Italy: it was the only theater where there were so many specialized "mountain" divisions. Employed mainly on the plains, these mountain divisions exhausted themselves in an infantry role when their expertise would have been better placed in the mountains of Italy, as much offensively as defensively. But in an army steeped only in notions of mechanized warfare, this fact was not understood.

Surrounded by partisans, German representatives from the various encircled units, especially 8.GD, negotiate their surrender to an American unit in the Po Valley. (DR)

From July to October 1942, Polizei-Gebirgsjäger-Regiment 18 was engaged in anti-partisan operations in Slovenia before transfer to Finland. (Reenactment with period items)

Operations Zone Adria-Küstenland (OZAK), 1943–45

This link between the Italian theater and the Balkans, the "operational zone of the Adriatic coast" (OZAK), was constituted when Italy changed sides on September 10, 1943. Several mountain units were engaged in this group. This theater of operations, up until then an Italian zone of occupation, comprised the Frioul, Görz, Trieste, Istria, Fiume (Rijecka), Quarnero, and Slovenia/Ljubljana (Laibach). The operational commander was *General der Gebirgstruppe* Ludwig Kübler. The structure became LXXXXVII.AK, stationed at Trieste, on September 28 1944.

This sector had a particularly important strategic role: logistics and transport routes cut through its core right into Reich territory (in this case, the Ostmark, formerly Austria), Although territorially the sector was not that large, the risks of an Allied landing, especially on the Istria Peninsula, were present in the minds of the planners. Resistance movements in the area were powerful, well structured, and well equipped. In 1942, a special mountain unit had been engaged in Slovenia, Polizei-Gebirgsjäger-Regiment 18 (see the chapters "The Balkans, and Crete, 1941" in *German Mountain Troops 1939–42* and "The Balkans, 1942–45," the next chapter in this volume).

Intended originally for the Caucasus and before transfer to the Karelia Front, this unit, the only "real" specialized mountain police regiment, took part in anti-

When training, the *Jäger* of Karstwehr-Bataillon wore cloth dress or fatigues with an earlier black *Kragenspiel*, then the universal SS runic. In combat the Karstwehr-Bataillon wore a cloth smock or fatigues, or only the shirt in warmer weather. The vertical slits for internal access on the camouflaged M42 smock were replaced by buttoned hip pockets. (Private collection)

This anti-partisan operation is being carried out by units of varying origins, among which are probably some *Karstjäger*.

partisan operations in Upper Krajina and Upper Carniole (Oberkrain) from July to October 1942. It was operational again in November before moving to Danzig by rail at the beginning of December, then Finland at the end of the month by sea.

On July 10, 1942, in order to suppress partisan activity in the Carso (Karst) on the borders of Italy, Austria (Ostmark), and Yugoslavia, the SS-Wehrgeologenkorps (Military Geologists' Corps of the SS) created a company made up mainly of *Volkdeutsche* Italians, Croats, and Slovenes at Dachau training camp, which became a 500-man battalion in November 1942, the SS.Karstwehr-Bataillon.

After combat training (*Mittel-* and *Hochgebirgskarstausbildung*), in medium- and high-altitude mountains of the Karst zone, the unit took part in a scientific expedition (Sonderkommando K[2]) in the Caucasus in September 1942. Its first major mission was disarming Italian troops in the Tarvisio region, where three borders met, and which became one of the focal points of Italian Resistance. The XVII sector of the Guardia alla Frontiera (fortress border units), the GaF, refused to lay down their arms and were attacked by young Karstwehr recruits: several were killed. Their keenness earned them the name "Black Devils" from the local populace.

The battalion, based at Gradisca d'Isonzo, then took part in several anti-partisan operations in the Trieste, Udine, and Istria regions, sustaining heavy losses between October 1943 and June 1944. It used a mix of Italian and German equipment. A police unit, Polizei-Freiwilligen-Gebirgsjäger-Bataillon Tagliamento—the initial uniform seems to have been Italian, then German with a "Polizei" armband and an edelwiss on the sleeve and the cap—was also active in the Frioul region; it had evolved from the Friaul-Freiwilligen-Regiment Tagliamento, with the same ethos as the Karstwehr, with 1,500 men recruited locally.

At the end of October and during November, the battalion took part in a series of operations among which was Operation *Traufe* (*Gutter*) in the Saga and Karfreit (Kobarid in Slovenian, Caporetto in Italian) regions, under command of Sicherungs-Gruppe von le Fort.

It worked with other mountain units, such as Gebirgsjäger-Ersatz-und Ausbildungs-Regiment 139, Gebirgsjäger-Bataillon Heine, or Reserve-Gebirgs-Artillerie-Regiment 112, which was organic to Reserve-Gebirgs-Division 188, based in Istria (Trieste) and which led most of the following operations: *Edelweiß* and *Enzian* (*Gentian*) in January/February 1944; *Ratte* (*Rat*) in February 1944; *Zypresse* (*Cypress*), *Märzveilchen* (*Violet*), *Maulwurf* (*Mole*), *Hellblau* (*Light Blue*), *Dachstein* (*Slate*), and *Osterglocke* (*Easter Bell*) in March 1944, in

2 Consituted by the Ahnenerbe, the Association for Research and Learning on Ancestral Heritage, a Nazi multidisciplinary research institute created by SS-Reichsführer Heinrich Himmler, Herman Wirth, and Walter Darré on July 1, 1935, it was incorporated into the SS in January 1939; the Ahnenerbe's headquarters were in Munich. The institute's objectives were the study of "the sphere, the spirit, the noble deeds and the patrimony of the Nordic Indo-European race" with, as tools, archaeological research, racial anthropology and the cultural history of the Aryan race. Its aim was to prove the validity of Nazi racial theories of the superiority of the Aryan race.

Osttürkischer Waffenverband der SS

The precursors of the Osttürkischer Waffenverband der SS were to be found in the units recruited during operations in the Caucasus (see earlier chapter "The Eastern Front, 1942–45"), locally, or in the PoW camps. The German command had two objectives: in the short term to establish forces motivated to fight against Bolshevism, and more generally by exploiting the resentment that the Eastern European peoples (*Ostvölker*) felt for the communist and atheist system which had caused such death and misery among the population during years of Soviet "reforms."

In the long term, and after they failed to occupy the North Caucasus, the Germans were counting on fomenting uprisings among the region's peoples, regrouped under one word, "Türken," to be understood as Turkish-speaking Muslims, but also including Armenians and Christian Georgians. (The Americans failed in their attempt to follow the same policy of subversion after the war with the same troops who had not been handed over to the Russians.)

By means of an order signed by the Reichsführer-SS on October 20, 1944, it was decided to create this *Waffenverband* with effect from October 1. The new unit was to assemble under its umbrella the *Osttürken*, Turkmen, Tatars of the Volga and the Urals, Turks from Crimea, Azeris, and others, originating for the most part from the regions to the north of the Caspian Sea. It was placed under command of a major of the Wehrmacht Heer, converted to Islam, who had served in the Austro-Hungarian and Turkish armed forces, incorporated as an *SS-Standartenführer*, Wilhelm Hintersatz, who had taken the name of Harun-al-Raschid Bey.

While preparing, the *Waffenverband* was assembled at Ruzomberk (Rosenberg) in Slovakia, an area that had been "cleansed" of Resistance movements beforehand. Initially the size of a regiment, it achieved a strength of 6,000 to 8,000, recruited primarily from the Waffen-SS but also from the Wehrmacht and the Polizei who had fought partisans, notably in eradicating the Polish Resistance in Warsaw.

The unit comprised a headquarters company and three battalions recruited ethno-linguistically: I.Btl. Turkmen; II.Btl. Tatars from the Idel-Ural region, very Islamized, with a project for a caliphate; and III.Btl. Azeris. These battalions were the basis for the subsequent regiments. Several mutinies, involving as much as a complete battalion, marked this preparation period, notably around Christmas 1944; but with the first rumblings, the command decided to organize things differently, in three *Waffengruppen* (assimilated regimental groupings): Idel-Ural, Turkestan, and Krim, each with two five-company battalions. The leftovers of the Ostmuselmanisches Regiment were included in the *Waffenverband*. At the same time, the Azeris left the Osttürkischer Waffenverband to join the Kaukasischer-Waffenverband der SS (KWVdSS) then being formed, and were replaced by the new Waffen-Gebirgs-Brigade der SS (Tatarische Nr. 1), itself derived from Waffen-Gebirgsjäger-Regiment der SS (Tatar. Nr. 1). The latter made up the Waffengruppe Krim. This reorganization was done in mid-January 1945, in Slovakia.

The national escutcheons of the Ostt.W-Verband der SS may have been worn, inherited from the Wehrmacht: Azerbaijan and Turkestan. (Private collections)

On an impulse, Colonel Hintersatz converted to Islam as Harun-al-Raschid-Bey, and a new Muslim unit was created which became the Osttürkischer Waffenverband der SS. This series of color shots is from an exceptional film made by Spiegel TV. It shows the variety of uniforms, in particular the headdress, cloths and turbans (in principle, a Muslim will not wear a hat with a peak). The imam is leading the prayer of the unit which was presented by Hintersatz himself to the "chaplain"; the closeup shows that he is wearing the SS rune on the collar and the epaulettes of an officer and not a *Sonderführer* (literally Special Leader, a civilian attached to the military), unlike his counterparts in the 13.(mus.) Waffen-Division Handschar. (Spiegel TV)

It was in fact incorporating this Tatar *Gebirgs-Brigade* that elevated the Osttürkischer Waffen-Verband (OTWVdSS) into the category of the major mountain units. The name of the OTWVdSS was to have been appended with "Timur" (Tamerlane) at the beginning of 1945 with four *Waffengruppen*: Azerbaischan, Turkestan, Krim, and Idel-Ural. The insignia planned for the left-hand *Kragenspiegel* was a wolf's head. The title of the KWVdSS would have been "Schamil" also with four *Waffengruppen*: Azerbaischan, Georgien, Nordkaukasus, and Armenien. The *Kragenspiegel* was to have borne the sword and the shield.

With the 8. Armee reserve until the end of March 1945, OTWVdSS deployed to Lombardy in the Milan region, and then Merate, 20 kilometers farther north. It committed the Waffengruppe Turkistan to limited anti-partisan operations, in the Modena province. Further desertions, with attempts to reach Switzerland, ended in bloody fashion. The remnants surrendered to the US 1st Armored Division at Rimini. Most of these volunteers were handed over to the Soviets.

The *Feldbluse* of an *SS-Unterscharführer* (sergeant) in the *Panzerjäger* of Ostt.W-Verband der SS, with the theoretical positioning of the insignia and a closeup of a cuff title. It is unclear if this was ever issued. (Private collection)

Osttürkischer Waffen-Verband der SS

The customs service created reaction units which contributed to the anti-partisan struggle near frontiers. The customs officers are wearing the insignia of their service with the Heer edelweiss on the *Bergmütze* and the *Feldbluse*. Two of them are wearing *Windjacke* cut from Italian cloth. (DR)

Karst and Istria; *Braunschweig* (*Brunswick*) end April/early May 1944, with notably Polizei-Regimenter 15 Bozen, whose personnel often wore an edelweiss; *Liane* in May, and *Annemarie* from May 7–June 16. These operations lasted between several days and several weeks and took place on an order from Field Marshal Kesselring to implement "an anti-partisan week." The battalion's best men were regrouped in a *Hochgebirgs-Kompanie*.

In August 1944, in accordance with an order from Himmler dated July 18, the battalion became a division with the designation 24. Waffen-Gebirgs-Division der SS Karstjäger, but with only 6,000 men on strength. As a major unit, *Karstjäger* could lead operations which of course the *Karstwehr* could not. With its classic structure, included was an armored company like those assigned to the light infantry divisions, equipped with Italian Carro Armato P40 tanks. Alongside its *Volksdeutsche*, this recently formed division even incorporated 150 Spaniards, the remainder of the Spanische-Freiwilligen-Legion, a group of SS volunteers who remained in Germany after the Azul Division (250.ID) returned to Spain. "Cleansing" operations continued during this period. *SS-Gruppenführer* (Lieutenant General) Odilo Globocnik[3] summoned the first recipients of the anti-partisan struggle insignia, the *Bandenkampfabzeichen*, to Tolmino on September 1, 1944, and from September 26–30, 1944, the new division was engaged on Operation *Klagenfurt* against the "free zone of east Frioul," the partisan term for the area.

From October 8–22, Operation *Waldläufer* (*Forest Runner*) resulted in the "free zone of Carniole and Frioul" being reabsorbed. In the town of Nimis, 452 houses were destroyed, six civilians killed and 28 deported in reprisals. In November 1944, 157.Res.-Div. was ordered to reinforce OZAK in Istria, but was directed to Italy (as above).

On December 6, facing difficulties with recruiting, the division was reduced to a brigade, the Waffen-Gebirgs-(Karstjäger)-Brigade, the designation it bore until February 10, 1945. On the 11th, it became 24. Waffen-Gebirgs-(Karstjäger) Division der SS until

3 This divisional commander, born in Trieste, was one of the earliest Austrian Nazis. A zealous organizer of the genocide in Poland, aimed at exterminating the Jews, he was captured by the British in 1945, but managed to commit suicide.

The anti-partisan struggle meant alternating between offensive operations and guarding installations. These MG gunners and guards could be *Karstjäger* or *Gebirgs-Polizisten*, given the color of their uniforms.

DIE WEHRMACHT

A major but relatively unknown unit, 188.GD was largely equipped with uniforms made from Italian camouflage cloth, as per the cover of *Die Wehrmacht*. The lace-up jacket is a copy of the Waffen-SS M40 smock; it was worn in other units of the Heer and the Luftwaffe, and even the Waffen-SS, as were the *Feldbluse* and the *Einheitsfeldmütze*. (Private collection)

the end of the war. It continued with minor operations against partisans and reprisals against the civilian population in the Julian Alps. On March 19, 1945, the unit began a series of operations, *Frühlingsanfang* (*Start of Spring*) and *Winterende* (*End of Winter*) under command of the *Stab*, as part of OZAK's anti-partisan struggle.

The launch of the Allied offensive toward the Po Valley along the Adriatic coast precipitated a general withdrawal, notably toward OZAK then toward the foothills of the Alps (*Alpenvorland*). *Karstjäger* fell back in order along the Tagliamento up to Osoppo and Gemona, forced back by the British and the New Zealanders, and harassed by partisans and *Jabos*. Finally, within Kampfgruppe Harmel,[4] it took part in the defense of the Karawanken Passes in the Julian Alps, between Slovenia and Austria, axes that were vital for the German forces retreating from Italy and Yugoslavia. The division surrendered to the British 6th Armored Division on May 9, 1945 between Tarvisio in Italy and Arnoldstein in Austria.

Anti-partisan operations *Bandenkampfabzeichen* insignia created on January 30, 1944, retroactive to January 1, 1943.

LXXXXVII.AK (Lieutenant General Ludwig Kübler) was engaged in the Fiume region with 188.GD, a training division, underequipped and not mobile, and 237.ID, a security division, unprepared for large-scale operations. The corps was ordered to attack from Trieste toward Rijeka (Fiume), facing an enemy that vastly outnumbered it. 188.GD held its position to the north and east of Fiume, then tried to break through northward to reach the Tagliamento, facing British units reinforced by partisans. Eight hundred and eighty missing never came back, no doubt massacred, like tens of thousands of German and Croat soldiers after the fighting. The division surrendered to the Soviets which had broken through to the Adriatic coast with the help of Tito's partisans. Kübler was seriously wounded on May 1 and replaced by Lieutenant General Hans Wilhelm von Hößlin (Colonel Christl succeeded him at the head of 188.GD). The corps surrendered to Yugoslav forces on May 5, 1945. Few survived captivity.

---

4 *SS-Brigadeführer* (Brigadier General) Heinz Harmel, as commander of the Frundsberg Division, had refused to carry out an order that would have caused the destruction of his unit and was transferred to this battlegroup as a punishment.

SS-Obersturmführer (First Lieutenant) Helmuth Prasch, company commander in 24. Waffen-Gebirgs Division der SS Karstjäger wearing the gold *Bandenkampfabzeichen*.

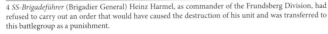

The first major mountain unit engaged in the Balkans during occupation by the Germans and Italians was the Freiwilligen-Gebirgs-Division der Waffen-SS, from October 1942. Its first commander was *SS-Brigadeführer und Generalmajor der Waffen-SS* Artur Phleps. He could not wear the Odal rune on his collar so he wore that of the Rasse-und Siedlungshauptamt (Central Administration for Race and Population) on his left-hand sleeve, using the same symbols. (DR)

The Balkans, 1942–45

Following the defeat of Greece and Yugoslavia in April/May 1941 (see chapter "The Balkans, and Crete, 1941" in Volume 1), the Balkan Peninsula was placed under a strict occupation regime relying on puppet governments. Yugoslavia was thus dismembered and divided up.

Germany took Carinthia, High Carniole, and southern Styria; Italy took West Slovenia (Ljubljana province), the coastal district of Dalmatia, and Montenegro (declared "independent"); Albania took Kosovo, and the western portion of Macedonia; Hungary took Voïvodina (districts of Prekmurje, Medjimurje, Baranjska, and Backa with large Hungarian minorities); Bulgaria took eastern Serbia.

Besides, Croatia-Slavonia, Dalmatia, and Bosnia-Herzegovina formed the independent state of Croatia. Finally, Serbia, more or less within its 1912 borders, came directly under German military administration, with a puppet government of "national salvation" under General Milan Nedic. The Banat, the northernmost point of Serbia, to the north of Pančevo, was, practically, administered by *Volkdeutsche*, who were well embedded in the region (the *Donauschwaben*, Schwabs of the Danube).

Greece suffered the same fate as Serbia.

The Germans engaged in a merciless struggle against the partisans in the Balkans, using as far as possible local resources to collaborate alongside or within the Wehrmacht

The 7. SS-Freiwilligen Gebirgs-Division Prinz Eugen's first engagement showed the limits of deploying a major unit which had not been properly formed. As with the *Div. Stab*, a number of personnel still wore the runic SS. (DR)

The SS worn on the chest and the *Kragenspiegel* of a Prinz Eugen officer, the Odal rune. (Private collection)

(Heer but also Luftwaffe ground forces), the Waffen-SS, and Polizei. The extent of the territories they had to hold onto, or at least control and secure, the features of the terrain, respecting the alliances, the partisans' different political characters (each had contradictory postwar goals)—all these led to the constitution of complex and volatile systems of command.

Note that the strategic interest in the Balkans was not just military: with deposits of bauxite (Mostar), chrome (Demotos), copper, lead and zinc (Trepča), coal, iron and oil, these were raw materials that were vital for the German war effort, which goes some way in explaining the way in which they held onto the peninsula.

Yugoslavia

The Yugoslav theater was the only one, according to the veterans, where even the medics had to carry a weapon, unable to take advantage of the temporary neutrality their Red Cross armbands afforded them. The partisans' ethos was that they could not take prisoners as they had no camps to put them in, and the occupiers reciprocated. The methods used by both sides were therefore marked by extreme savagery, to be found in other wars, notably in Bosnia-Herzegovina, the "country of hate" of the 1980s and 1990s. In Albania conditions were similar, in a state supposedly sovereign, but in fact under Italian domination, supported by the Germans.

In Greece, the influence of the British, through the numerous instructors (including Randolph, Winston Churchill's own son) limited this savagery, but the communist influence was stronger there than elsewhere and committed the country to a cruel civil war after the conflict.

In the end, the partial collapse of the Eastern Front in the summer of 1944 was to lead to a significant breakthrough by the Red Army toward Yugoslavia, territory ultimately freed by Tito's forces, renamed the Yugoslav National Army, the JNA (the name used until the breakup of the country in 1992).

Although a few Yugoslav units were able to escape the country before the German invasion, for Egypt (the future Army of Liberation, or of the Exterior) and join King Petar

Two Prinz Eugen officers during a ceremony for the award of the Iron Cross 2nd Class. Both wear the escutcheon with two runes (showing that they come from the SS) on the *Feldbluse* chest with a dark green, bluish collar, with slanting hip pockets (a cut inherited from the SS-VT uniforms). They are already wearing the division's escutcheon, the Odal rune, on the collar and the Prinz Eugen cuff title. The *SS-Untersturmführer* (second lieutenant) on the right is Dr Victor Brack who served in the Prinz Eugen from August 1943 to July 1944 and who was the instigator of the Aktion T4 euthanasia program which led to the elimination of 300,000 mentally and physically disabled people as well as the sterilization of Jews who were fit for work. He was hanged in 1948 for crimes against humanity. (DR, colorized by V. Lopatin)

II (Peter Karageorgevitch), internally, resistance developed quickly, in two significant movements. Firstly, as early as May 9, 1941, Colonel Dragoljub "Draža" Mihailović created the Chetnik detachments, recognized later by the king as the Yugoslav Army in the country, which numbered some 72,000 combatants and perhaps 200,000 reservists. Its HQ was installed the same day in the village of Ravna Gora, in the eponymous mountains in the center of Serbia, in Sumadija, a region which had been freed from the Ottoman yoke. Their operations took place mostly in Serbia, in Bosnia-Herzegovina, Montenegro, Slovenia, and Macedonia. The Chetniks were monarchists, pro-Allies, and anti-communist.

This last characteristic caused circumstantial, makeshift alliances between local chiefs and the German and Italian occupiers. The Italians had ambiguous relations with these partisans—the Italians armed anti-Tito partisans—about which in early March 1943 the Germans wanted clarification. The Germans did consider disarming the partisans, with the threat of action if German interests were imperiled.

After Germany had broken the Molotov–Ribbentrop pact by attacking the Soviet Union, Josip Broz "Tito," a Croat and Communist agent, created the partisan detachments which became the Yugoslav Army of Liberation in November 1942. Aligned with the policy of developing Communism in as many countries as possible as decreed by Moscow, Tito's objective was to set up a Communist government in his country after expelling the Germans and evicting the monarchists. In addition to the occupation, this could only lead to civil war.

We have seen in the chapter "The Balkans, and Crete, 1941" in *German Mountain Troops 1939–42* that Yugoslavs seized weapons from the Kragujevac arsenal (near Ravna Gora), the beginning of a form of resistance. Yugoslavia was quickly overrun in April 1941: the Communists had acted with the "oppressed" minorities to encourage defeatism, to support secessionist ideas already prevalent among these minorities, which brought about the quick surrender of the Croats and the Slovenes, notably with arms and baggage trains. Allied support was rapidly forthcoming, from Great Britain at first to Mikhailovich before deciding to drop him in August 1942. The British gradually gave up supporting the Resistance as a whole, leaving the Soviets to support Tito, thereby preparing for the future. The Americans then supported the Chetniks but abandoned them in 1944.

Occupying this very compartmentalized country—with mostly mountainous regions, very closed-in valleys, rivers that were difficult to cross, impenetrable forests, and populated by people toughened by the inhospitable land they lived in—was reduced to controlling the

The principal piece of the Gebirgs-Artillerie-Regiment Prinz Eugen was the Skoda 7.5cm Model 15 howitzer, with or without the shield.

1.GD arriving by rail in the Balkans having come from the Kuban Front. All routes were used for transporting supplies to the forces engaged in the peninsula. As soon as it unloaded from the trains, 1.GD deployed for Operation *Schwarz* (*Black*) on foot and by vehicle. (Franz Moll Archives)

towns and the main axes and by specific operations, of varying import depending on the size of the enemy bands. The occupation troops responsible for internal security were initially mostly Italian or local.

In June 1941, 12. Armee under Field Marshal List assigned LXV.AK under Lieutenant General Bader to occupy Serbia and part of Croatia, with headquarters in Belgrade. With the help of the 1st Bulgarian Army, second-rate German divisions carried out particularly bloody anti-partisan operations from September 1941 to February 1942. On March 1, 1942, LXV.AK became the Militärbefehlshaber Serbien (Serbian Military Command).

By the end of 1942, resistance activity had increased in Bosnia and decreased in Serbia. On November 16, a new HQ was created, the Befehlshaber der deutschen Truppen in Kroatien (Command German Troops in Croatia), under *General der Infanterie* Rudolf Lüters who had the Prinz Eugen as his primary subordinated unit from November 16, 1942 to August 24, 1943, the date at which it became XV.Geb.-AK.

Following an order dated January 13, 1942, Freiwilligen-Gebirgs-Division der Waffen-SS (7. SS-Freiwilligen-Gebirgs-Division Prinz Eugen from October 22, 1943) under Transylvanian Brigadier General Artur Phleps, joined Militärbefehlshaber Serbien in October. It comprised 15,000 *Volkdeutsche* from Banat, Romania, and Croatia, all volunteers

The principal Croat mountain units (*Legionsdivisionen*) received German instructors who sewed the Croat escutcheon under the edelweiss.

(*Freiwillige*[1]) and selected from outside the usual system, in particular by recruiting among the veterans of the Austro-Hungarian Army, some of whom had served in the Yugoslav Army. Phleps himself was himself a veteran of the Austro-Hungarian Army, and later the Romanian Army. The glorious name of Prinz Eugen, given on April 1, improved the image of the new division which based itself in southwestern Serbia where it was able to perfect its training and develop its cohesion, whilst carrying out security missions.

On July 17, 1942, Himmler gave a simple order: Dragoljub Mihailović was the major enemy in Yugoslavia (cited by the Communists after the war that he was not guilty of high treason). The evolution of the relative power of Tito's followers, supported by the Allies, especially by the USSR, naturally caused the entire strategic situation to shift.

The first operation involving the Prinz Eugen was launched on October 12, 1942, under command of BefH in Kroatien. The target was Commandant Dragutin Keserović, one of the "illegal" Chetnik personalities, identified as being in the Kopaonik Mountains, one of the highest Serbian ranges, around Kriva-Reka, on the border of Kosovo. This region was highly strategic, crisscrossed by major road and rail logistics axes, toward Greece and beyond, near the lead (used for making U-boat batteries) and zinc mines at Trepča, near Kosovo Mitrovica. The operation was a relative failure: Keserović managed to escape with most of his 1,500 men, but the operation did manage to iron out some command-and-control issues. Reprisals were carried out against the civilian population during the operation, in particular the 50 or so inhabitants (120 according to some sources) who were burned alive in the church at Kriva-Reka; an estimated total of 670 civilians were victims of the reprisals.

At the end of December 1942, 150,000 partisans were observed gathered to the west of Bosnia, in the Slunj–Knin–Travnik–Banja Luka quadrilateral, an area they considered as liberated.

On January 1, 1943, 12. Armee, positioned at Thessalonica, became Army Group E and included Mil.BefH.Serbien, the 1st Bulgarian Army, and Befh.Kroatien which commanded the Prinz Eugen. At the end of January, the Croat mountain divisions were changed to Kroatische Legionsdivisionen with German officers and NCOs, wearing *Gebirgstruppe* dress with German and Croat insignias, regrouped within an *Ausbildungs-Stab* per brigade.

Operation *Weiß I* through *III* (*White I* through *III*) were launched against Tito's troops and Titoists between January 20 and February 18, 1943 (*Weiß I*). The economic and operational aim of *Weiß* was repeated: prevent the enemy from occupying the bauxite mines (accounting for 10 percent of German aluminum requirements) at Mostar and push him back southward. Advancing along two axes with a *Kampfgruppe* on each, the Prinz Eugen came out at Karlovac then swung south (Slunj then Bihac) on the western flank of the operation in which five German divisions were engaged, facing the 8th and part of the 7th Partisan divisions. The weather was atrocious, the snow up to 1.2 meters (4 feet) deep. As they advanced, the Titoists who had not been attacked repositioned themselves behind

---

1 *Freiwilligen* was used ingeniously. This was the theory at least because initial recruitment failed to attract enough recruits, so much so that some units could not be constituted. Conscription in the Banat region (17–50-year-olds), however, ensured numbers were made up. In terms of officers, Phleps recruited from among his former Austro-Hungarian comrades; however, transfer to the Prinz Eugen was initially considered a punishment posting.

the advance elements and troops had to be taken out of the frontlines to secure the lines of communications against traps and ambushes.

At the beginning of March 1943, during *Weiß II*, the Prinz Eugen took part in the fighting, aimed at exploiting *Weiß I* in Croatia, by destroying the main Tito forces and thereby the Titoist state in the Glamoc–Livno–Bugojno–Jajce sector. The operation ended on March 20 with the bauxite mines occupied and the Communist forces to the north and west of the Narenta/Nerevta destroyed.

Weiß III, placed under Italian command, did not concern any German mountain units. The first serious confrontations between Titoists and Chetniks took place to the north of Knin in March 1943.

On April 8, Prinz Eugen set up strongpoints on the Mostar–Sarajevo logistics axis. On April 26 and 27, it strengthened its reconnoitering in the Livno–Ravno region and helped extricate an Ustase battalion encircled by Titoists and to "cleanse" the sector.

Operation *Schwarz* (*Black*) began on May 15, 1943, a large operation in Montenegro against "Draža," who since May 5 had been mobilizing his forces and was already celebrating the coming German defeat in Africa. The aim of the operation was to continue destroying Tito's forces and then, especially, annihilating the Chetniks, without revealing this intention to the Italians who supported them—this in order to eliminate a threat behind the Germans, in case of an Allied landing in the Balkans. Two mountain divisions were involved, Prinz Eugen to the west, and 1.GD to the east (having arrived in Montenegro in mid-April from the Kuban Front). 118.JgD advanced to the north, in parallel with the Prinz Eugen.

Elements of 1.GD reached Nič between April 4–18, advancing along the eastern pincer. On May 8, two battalions from the division were sent from Novi Pazar and Mitrovica toward Tuitin and Rakos. The next day, while advancing towards Berane, a hundred or so Chetniks were captured and disarmed. On the 12th, the *Vorausabteilungen* continued their advance towards Bjelo Polje (63 kilometers to the southwest of Novi Pazar) and Andrijevica. *Jagdkommandos* "cleansed" hostile elements along the way. On May 15, the division encountered Communists and alleged it had approached the Chetniks.

The Prinz Eugen started off from Mostar on May 15 faced with an uncomfortable situation: the Italians were supporting the withdrawing Chetniks and refused to establish liaison detachments with the Prinz Eugen. On the 16th, 1.GD reached the Kolašin–Blatina region and captured 2,000 Chetniks after repelling Titoists to the west. The weather was overcast, preventing the Luftwaffe from properly intervening. On the 18th, the division continued its advance west (Mojkovac on the northern axis, the heights west of Kolašin on the southern axis), pushing back the enemy trying to hold ground. Brandenburg Regiment 1 took part in the "cleansing" behind 1.GD, which was closing the net eastward on May 19, and then the crest line to the west-southwest of Kolašin and Lipovo, against Titoists who fell back after they'd held out with some determination. One last act of resistance, on the *Sperr-linie*, was dealt with on the 20th. The Prinz Eugen had not yet come into contact with the enemy and was advancing east-southeast.

On May 19, most of the "legal" Chetniks had been disarmed and evacuated to the south of Montenegro by the Italians, covered by 1.GD.

On the 31st, with Luftwaffe support, the Prinz Eugen pushed back significant numbers of Chetniks and Titoists toward the Piva (a tributary of the Drina, 20 kilometers northwest of Foca), toward the Durmitor range and the defensive line of 1.GD, and Šavnik (24 kilometers northwest of Niksic). Kampfgruppe Schmidthuber (SS-GJR2) reached Podgorica without contacting the enemy. Kampfgruppe Hahn (II./SS-GJR1) found itself encircled by strong Chetnik and Titoist elements in the Lisna-Gora, 17 kilometers to the east of Gacko. The Prinz Eugen advance continued on the 22nd. Titoists attacked Chetnik positions.

On May 24, four to six Communist brigades tried to break through north, in front of 118.JgD, then stopped and consolidated on the Drina between Foča and Goražde. The next day, liaison was established between 118.JgD and the Prinz Eugen whilst Kampfgruppe Hahn disengaged. On the 26th, Titoist units—among which apparently was Tito's HQ—increased pressure on the heights to the south of the Drina.

On May 27, fighting increased in intensity in the Prinz Eugen's sector. On the right wing, I. and II./SS-GJR1 attacked where resistance was weak. On the left, I., III., and IV./SS-GJR2 made contact on the heights to the southwest of Bakilj and to the north-northwest of Šavnik.

Once the enemy had been stopped, 1.GD resumed its advance on the flank, west and northwest so as to tighten the noose. 118.JgD resumed its advance to the south of the Drina toward Vučevo. About two or three brigades of Titoists appeared to be regrouping to break out westward, from the Žabljak region to the north of Šavnik.

118.JgD and 1.GD continued their advance respectively toward the south and the northwest. On May 31, while elements had advanced on foot up until then, in order to secure the area, the Prinz Eugen quickly organized its resources by vehicle in the Gacko–Tjentište–Zabljak–Šavnik quadrilateral. On June 1, 1.GD approached the sector from Šavnik, and 118.JgD from the northwest (Tjentište). The enemy had concentrated around Mratinje, half way between Pluzine and Vučevo, in order to break out west. Hand-to-hand fighting broke out, with the Titoists even managing to encircle some German units.

In the days that followed, the Germans tried to reduce the pockets of resistance while attempting to prevent the Communist partisans exfiltrating to the northwest (Jeleč and Kalinovic especially), a rugged and wooded region, then into the Durmitor range. By taking the bridges across the Piva, the Prinz Eugen had considerably hindered the Titoists' movements and logistics. Their last elements found themselves halted to the west of the river in an area blocked to the north and which was being progressively reduced from the south. 1.GD discovered many civilians dead from typhus and burned their villages, at the same time freeing hundreds of Italian soldiers who had been taken prisoner by the Titoists.

Schwarz was considered finished on June 15, 1943. Skirmishes finished off the last bits of resistance, but the *GDen* did not give chase to any escapees. The Prinz Eugen regrouped in the Gacko–Avtovac sector, and then returned to Mostar, now able to secure the bauxite mines as well as carrying out operations to secure the axes; the bulk of the division centered on Sarajevo where it set up its command post. Phleps handed over command of the division to Brigadier General Reichsritter von Oberkampf.

On June 19, 1.GD set off toward northern Greece (Florina). At the end of the month, it reached the Ioannina sector in Epirus. In July and August 1943, a Prinz Eugen *Kampfgruppe*

Finding itself in a medium mountain milieu, 1.GD has sent its *Reiter* (riders) from Geb.-Aufkl.-Abt.54 out on reconnaissance. The Prinz Eugen also had riders in its reconnaissance battalion. (Franz Moll Archives)

These two radio operators from the Prinz Eugen have received a message by motorcycle dispatch rider. They are going to convert it into an optical message via the Lichtsprechgerät 80 (the luminophone, the modern version of the heliograph) which they have camouflaged behind a makeshift wall (the hardness of the karstic ground precluded any digging of foxholes). This apparatus, made by Carl Zeiss in Jena from 1937 onward, enabled radio messages transformed into light rays to be sent and received, by day with a white light or with a red filter, and by night with an infrared filter. (LEX Colorization)

These *Jäger* from the Prinz Eugen are probably taking part in Operation *Geiserich* in September 1943; some units were brought in by air. (DR)

took part in minor operations against aggressive *Banden* around Sarajevo. At the end of August/early September, hundreds of Croats of all ranks deserted and joined the Titoists.

The Allied landings in Sicily in July 1943 had lifted any doubts about where the Second Front was going to take place, but it was inevitably going to cause Italy to change sides. (The Germans had been fearful of Allied landings in the Balkans.) Among the measures taken as part of Operation *Achse* (*Axe*), which treated this development as significant, the reorganization of the region's command in August 1943 has to be mentioned. Army Group F under Field Marshal Maximilian von Weichs, with its HQ in Belgrade, took over control of all Axis forces in the Balkans: 2. Panzerarmee (ex-Eastern Front), and BefHbr Serbien, which became MilBefh Südost (Southeast Military Command, now almost entirely Bulgarian). The operational components were 2.PzA under Lieutenant General Lothar Rendulic, with its command post at Kragujevac but with no armored divisions; XV.Geb.-AK (ex-Mil BefH in Kroatien) with two infantry divisions (369., and 373.), one *Jäger* (114) and the Prinz Eugen; and LXIX.Res.AK, XXI.Geb.AK (whose divisions were not mountain divisions: 100, 118. JgD, and 297.ID). Note that the *Jäger* divisions (formerly infantry) were equipped for the mountains but did not wear the insignia. When Italian troops were disarmed in Croatia and in Montenegro during Operation *Achse*, the Prinz Eugen ran into difficulties around Split with Italian troops who had changed sides.

Put on alert the previous day, on September 8, 1943, the Prinz Eugen met resistance from the partisans and the Italians, who had armor and artillery support. On September 10, Rgts.-Gruppe 2 (*SS-Obersturmbannführer*, or Lieutenant Colonel, Schmidhuber) pushed on toward Ragusa (Dubrovnik) where the Italian IV Corps refused to surrender. After an attack by Stukas the regiment occupied the town and captured 30,000 Italians. Kampfgruppen Groß and Meckelburg ran into similar difficulties. In Montenegro the Taurinese Division went over lock, stock and barrel to the partisans. II./SS-GJR2 (*SS-Sturmbannführer*, or Major, Dietsche) captured the port at Ploce that had been sabotaged by the Italians before being handed over to the partisans. Among the Italians, only the volunteers—mainly Black Shirts—were accepted as allies of the Germans, the rest being incarcerated in PoW camps. SS-GJR1 (Lieutenant Colonel Petersen) fought bitterly against the partisans and the Italians at Split, suffering significant losses, especially to the south of the port, near the Klis fortress.

II./SS-GJR1 (Major Breimaier) was encircled and almost captured after losing more than 50 killed and 120 wounded. To extricate this unit and regain the initiative in this sector, XV.Geb.-AK committed successive elements, mostly brought in by Ju 52s under fire, after September 23—II./SS-GJR2 first, then I./SS-GJR1, and finally the rest of GJR1 as well as various other units, including IR (mot.) 92 (who inherited the traditions of the Orientkorps)—as part of Operation *Geiserich*, placed under command of von Oberkamp. Following this fortnight of uninterrupted fighting, Petersen became the division's third holder of the Knight's Cross. Once Split and its surrounds were *in deutscher Hand*, the division "cleansed" the Dalmatian coast (due to the renewed fears of an Allied landing). However, the partisans reoccupied the area as soon as the Germans left.

On October 22, the Prinz Eugen was allocated the number 7 in the order of battle and its regiments were numbered accordingly. From October 23 to November 11, 1943, the division carried out three smaller operations to secure the coast and to support the Ustase: *Herbstgewitter* (*Autumn Storm*), *Landsturm* (*Land Assault*), and *Seeräuber* (*Pirate*).

This 1.GD battalion command post is engaged in anti-partisan operations in the Dubrovnik sector. The Tornister-Funkgerät radio is clearly visible. (*Die Wehrmacht*)

A new division appeared, under command of *SS-Brigadeführer* (Brigadier General) Sauberzweig, 13.(mus.) Waffen-Division Handschar. It was assembled in France (see following chapter "The Campaign in the West, 1944–45") and at Sennelager. (Colorization)

In September 1943, SS-GJR1 was confronted with Titoist partisans and Italian soldiers who had joined them after Italy changed sides. This *SS-Oberscharführer* (technical sergeant) on the cover of *Die Wehrmacht* is engaged in the Split region.

The Grand Mufti of Jerusalem, a fierce opponent of the British and the Jews since the 1920s, contributed significantly in recruiting Muslims throughout the Balkans. (Bundesarchiv 101i-82-12-15)

V.SS-Gebirgs-Armee-Korps, constituted in Berlin on July 8, 1943, reached Yugoslavia in October, with its commanding general, Brigadier General Phleps, the former commander of the Prinz Eugen. On October 26, it linked up with XV.Geb.-AK with notably the Prinz Eugen as well as 13.(mus.) Waffen-Division Handschar, being trained under command of Brigadier General Karl-Gustav Sauberzweig. Its operational area covered the east of Bosnia, Herzogovina and most of Dalmatia, including the islands; the main worry was logistics, the only railway line being regularly cut by partisans.

1.GD was been dispatched to Florina in the north of Greece, at the beginning of November 1943, before continuing to the Kosovo, Mitrovica, and Novi Pazar, where it prepared for Operation *Kugelblitz* (*Lightning Ball*, or *St. Elmo's Fire*). Planning was so fast that the winter equipment did not have time to reach the division: it was sorely missed because heavy snows soon arrived, with the temperature dropping to 14°F. The weather, as well as the destroyed bridges, made movement difficult.

The sixth anti-partisan offensive, Operation *Kugelblitz*, commenced on December 2, 1943 in the east of Bosnia and in Croatia. The operation, delayed because of Italy switching sides, had German units confronting enemy forces that greatly outnumbered them, compared with what they were used to. The Prinz Eugen, 1.GD, and 2.Rgt. Brandenburg took part, alongside other German, Bulgarian, and indigenous divisions, facing four divisions of Tito's partisans assembled in the Rogatica–Vlasenica region (southeast of Bosnia).

The Prinz Eugen did not get off to a good start: its commander, worn out, requested leave and was granted it (Schmidhuber took over command of the division and Dietsche of SS-GJR14). A number of *Jäger* had to have their feet cared for, seriously affected by weeks of cold humidity. Operations started with 1.GD on the Sandžak, in the Prijpolje–Pljevlja region, then continued to the east of Sarajevo in order to prevent, successfully as it

These photos were most likely taken during Operation *Kugelblitz* (*Lightning Ball*) in southeastern Bosnia. These Italian prisoners had joined Tito's partisans in September 1943. The unit is either 1.GD or 2.Rgt. Brandenburg (both units wore the same uniform). (ECPAD)

transpired, the assembled Titoists advancing on this key town. *Kugelblitz* continued after December 18, 1943, with a second phase, Operation *Schneesturm* (*Snowstorm*), against the partisans who had fallen back toward the north-northwest, in order to disperse, eliminate or capture enemy forces halted in the first phase. Among the prisoners were 1,900 Italians who had gone over to the Communist partisans in September 1943. Christmas Day was particularly trying with heavy losses, the units exhausted by the difficulty in moving about, the hand-to-hand fighting against a motivated enemy, and all in the snowed-over Dinaric Alps. On December 27, the order to halt was received: units rested, leaving patrols to reconnoiter the enemy. At the same time, XV.Geb.-AK had "cleansed" the island of Korcula, off the Dalmatian coast.

Operation *Waldrausch* (*Noises of the Forest*), from January 4–18, 1944, took place to the west of the Travnik–Kupreš–Glamoč region. It was carried out by V.SS-Gebirgs-Armee-Korps with 1.GD—from the Knin area—and the Prinz Eugen. Tito managed to escape the pocket before it was encircled by German forces. The harsh winter mountain conditions (up to two meters of snow), the absence of roads and inadequate logistics, ultimately called for an extended recovery period. Almost eight weeks of non-stop fighting in extreme conditions incurred a cost. I./SS-GJR13, outflanked by a massive enemy attack, almost fled the field, sustaining heavy losses, its men having given up. SS-GJR13 (recently taken over by Major Vollmer, former commander of I./SS-GJR13) was declared inoperative. In January, losses amounted to almost 6,000 men.

At the end of *Waldrausch*, Colonel Otto Kumm succeeded von Oberkamp (appointed Inspector of Mountain Troops in the SS-FHA) at the head of the Prinz Eugen. Almost all the commanders were changed and, in his operational area, the Sarajevo region, and until April 1944, Kumm conducted small-scale operations, *Jagdkommandos*, to make it easier for the new COs to get their units into shape.

1.GD was ordered to the southeast of Zagreb (Agram) on foot, across excessively rough terrain, made almost impenetrable by the icy rain and the snow (up to four meters deep). It reached its new operational area in early March 1944 to prepare for a new task, anticipating Hungary's defection. To do this, after traversing the country with its officers reassured as to the loyalty of their Magyar soldiers, 1.GD reinforced its mountain units engaged in the Carpathian passes—from Uzkoser to the north of Ghimes in Transylvania—where Soviet armored vanguards were already starting to break through. After stabilizing the situation and leaving 8. Armee to take over responsibility for the sector, the division set off again for Greece.

In early 1944, 2.Regiment Brandenburg was detached to V.SS-Gebirgs-Armee-Korps, in the Prijpolje region, on the Sandžak (just west of Montenegro). Reinforced by Bosnian militias and from time to time Serbian Chetniks, it took part in securing the axes and in lesser operations to retake ground. The commander of I./2. Rgt. Brandenburg, Captain Kurt Konrad Steidl, facing two Titoist brigades which had settled in the area, captured the bridge at Prijpolje, set up a bridgehead and held it until reinforcements arrived. He was awarded the Knight's Cross on January 26, 1944.

Having finished its preparation and training in France (Villefranche de Rouergue), then in Germany (Neuhammer, in Silesia), 13.SS-Geb.-Frw.-Div. carried out a series of

Säuberungsaktionen (cleansing operations) at regimental and battalion level, alternating with major operations under command of the army corps, as seen below. These took place during the spring and the summer of 1944, in the west of Bosnia where Himmler had confined it to a *Sicherheitszone* (safety zone), allowing the division only rarely to operate outside this zone: Operation *Wegweiser* (*Signpost*) from March 10–12, to the north of the Save, around the Bosut woods; and Operation *Save* to the south of the eponymous river and in the corner formed by its confluence with the Drina, from March 15–26.

Operation *Osterei* (*Easter Egg*) took place between the Drina and Lopare, on April 12. After the fighting, I./SS-GJR28 with Albanian recruits, left the Handschar and went by train to join the 21. SS-Gebirgs-Division Skanderbeg whose assembly in Kosovo had been decided on the 17th by Himmler. This battalion was made up by drawing men from the support units and with new young recruits. Operation *Vollmond* (*Full Moon*) took place from June 7–12. Operation *Fliegenfänger* (*Flycatcher*), to the north of Osmaci, on July 14, aimed at capturing an aerodrome used by the Allies for resupplying the partisans. Operation *Heidrose* (*Moor Rose*) took place from July 17–19. Operation *Hackfleisch* (*Mincemeat*), within Operation *Rübezahl*,[2] took place from August 4–8.

On March 9, 1944, as it did at regular intervals, the OKW undertook a threat assessment in the Yugoslav theater, with a quantitative and qualitative estimate of enemy forces. It provided its forthright opinion on their operational value: the German forces were no longer confronted with *Banden* but structured units, well commanded, with modern heavy weapons, and motivated by effective command and control structures that enabled them to increase their strength and effectiveness.

At the end of March/early April, 1944, Tito attempted to occupy the town of Jajce which was contested by elements of the Prinz Eugen. In early May, 1.GD as *Feuerwehr* (fire brigade) from southeastern Europe returned to Yugoslavia by train, and disembarked to the north of Belgrade: the railway lines to Greece had been destroyed by Allied aircraft and the bridges over the Danube were continually being attacked. Then, via Macedonia along the roads, it reached Epirus, the Ionnina, the Adriatic coast, and the Albanian border. From May 3 to July 20, 1944, it carried out limited anti-partisan operations, such as at Metsovon or Argyrokastron, the Pindhos range, and in the south of Albania. The developing Yugoslav situation prompted the German command to deploy 1.GD to Montenegro and from there to Serbia. On July 25, its forward elements reached Mitrovica.

Operation *Maibaum* (*May Tree*), from April 26 to May 18, 1944, in two major phases, was the seventh large anti-partisan operation in the west of Bosnia, and consisted of attacking Titoist units as they regrouped to get the best results. The engagement of *Kampfgruppen* from 7. and 13. SS-GD—the baptism of fire for the latter—in the area to the east of Sarajevo encompassing Zvornik, Srebrnica, Goražde, the Drina, Pale, and Olovo, led initially to the equivalent of one Titoist division out of the three from the III Proletarian Corps being crushed. The 16th and 17th Communist Divisions gave up their objective of crossing the Drina; Tito remained to the east of Bosnia where he sustained heavy losses. Some partisans died of hunger soon after capture.

The Handschar engaged several *Jagdkommandos* from April 21–23 and fought in particular around Vlasenica and Šekovici, from April 21–May 1. The second phase,

---

2 Rübezahl was a giant in Central European legend, the master of lightning, a capricious spirit of the mountains.

The edelweiss on a black background, regulation for the Waffen-SS; the Prinz Eugen cuff band, woven by BEVo, decorated the sleeves of all 7. SS-Freiwilligen-Gebirgs-Division personnel. (Private collections)

Operation *Maiglöcken* (*Lily of the Valley*), commenced soon after. This operation consisted of chasing and destroying Titoist elements who had escaped from the *Jagdkommandos*, reinforced by Chetnik units, in the Majevica range.

Operation *Rösselsprung* (*Little Horse Jump*) was started right after Operation *Maibaum*. It was an attempt to capture Tito. Toward the end of February, a Brandenburg commando had located Tito's HQ, at Drvar, a large village at the end of a closed-in valley, in western Bosnia.

The fifth major operation against the partisans (Operation *Schwarz*) had forced Tito to abandon Jajce (100 kilometers northwest of Sarajevo) and to relocate 80 kilometers farther west. Given this information, V.SS-Gebirgs-Armee-Korps HQ (Phleps) commanding the operation, assisted by the commando Otto Skorzeny, examined several plans to destroy Tito. Only an airborne operation, with the surprise and speed such an action required, seemed to have any chance of succeeding. Three successive waves of SS-Fallschirmjäger-Bataillon 500, a semi-penal unit, jumped near the operational grotto where Tito was sheltering, together with Allied liaison groups. The battalion suffered heavy losses and was unable to capture the marshal who, it seems, had got wind of the operation. The Prinz Eugen cordoned off the northeast and the east until June 6 and destroyed several Titoist elements. Although *Rösselsprung* failed in its primary objective—capturing or killing Tito—it did disrupt his command and control for several months.

The Prinz Eugen extended *Rösselsprung* until the end of July 1944, pursuing isolated elements in a "free for all hunt" (*Freie Jagd*) between Kupres, Travnik, Zenica, Sarajevo, and Jablanica. The division's command post was attacked and partly destroyed, showing how in this theater there was no frontline and no rear. On May 10, 1944, Himmler announced to Phleps that he intended to establish two army corps, one in Bosnia, the other in Albania, with two divisions each, with a total of five divisions in all, including the Prinz Eugen and forming a predominantly Muslim "army."

It was Hitler who decided to establish the second "Croat" Muslim division on May 28, the 23. Waffen-Gebirgs-Division der SS (Kroatische Nr. 2) Kama. It was under command of Colonel Hellmuth Raithel (the future commander of SS-GJR28). It was delayed by Operation *Vollmond* but was operational by June 19 at Brčko.

IX. Waffen-Gebirgs-Korps der SS (Kroatisches) was constituted in Hungary on May 29, 1944 with effect from June 1. It was intended to include Bosno-Muslim units. Under command of Colonel Karl-Gustav Sauberzweig (who had handed over the Handschar to Desiderius Hampel on June 19), it was engaged as soon as it was ready against Titoist partisans and Chetniks, under command of 2. Panzer-Armee (with its command post at Kragucevac) in October and November.

The corps' ethos was defined in November 1944, encouraged by Sauberzweig: Bosnia was to become a Muslim entity, independent of the Communists who were beginning to

This Waffen-SS *Gebirgsjäger* is wearing the *Spielhahnstoß* (grouse feathers) of an Austrian *Alpenjäger* and the regulation SS death's head on his *Bergmütze*, in a non-regulation manner.

overrun the whole of former Yugoslavia; the Bosno-Muslim forces were to take part in the future control of the region. In December, the HQ joined 6. Armee in Hungary with some of its organic elements. It took part in the defense of Budapest until January 1945 when it was encircled; IV. Panzer-Korps' counterattack was unable to extricate it and it capitulated with 45,000 soldiers.

In July 1944, Major Oesterwitz took command of 2. Regiment Brandenburg. At the beginning of August its II. Bataillon took part in Operation *Rübezahl*, the major anti-partisan operation to the south of Sarajevo, the aim of which was to prevent Titoist partisans from controlling the Sandžak (very much Islamized) and the west of Montenegro; it was under command of V.SS-Gebirgs-Armee-Korps. This operation took place from August 5–22. The Prinz Eugen, 1.GD, and the Handschar were engaged in the first phase, as well as 21. SS-Gebirgs-Division Skanderbeg, recruited from Albanian-speaking Muslims that had its baptism of fire during Operation *Draufgänger* (*Daredevil*, part of *Rübezahl*), which very quickly revealed how unreliable its indigenous personnel were, ready to desert at the drop of a hat.

Tito seemed indeed to be making an effort to regroup his forces in Montenegro by organizing them strictly in battalions, regiments, brigades, divisions, and army corps, and equipping them with military uniforms, which were quite disparate, giving them more the look of a popular liberation army. Moreover, as well as captured German and Italian matériel,

Tito benefited from Allied support in heavy weapons—including armor and artillery of all calibers—plus American air support from Italy as well as effective radio means for good coverage of the battlefield and better command and control coordination. On August 22, 1944, Allied air forces succeeded in getting a thousand Titoist partisans out of the Durmitor range before they were captured by the Prinz Eugen and 1.GD advancing respectively from the north and south, to link up in the Durmitors.

In July 1944, Army Group Center collapsed and 20 or so divisions vanished from the Wehrmacht's order of battle. On August 23 there was another major disruption, this time on the edge of the Balkans: Romania changed sides, enabling the Red Army to accelerate their offensive toward Hungary

German Alpine *Jäger* operating in the Balkans, as seen on the cover of *Signal*.

These scenes of the Prinz Eugen fighting in anti-partisan operations were used by the propaganda services. (DR)

and the Yugoslav border. The anti-partisan struggle took another turn even before German forces were ordered to fall back from the Balkans to the Reich's borders on October 3. On the 8th, Bulgaria in turn declared war on Germany. From the 1st to the 7th, an increase in Allied pressure, aimed at the lines of communications (Operation *Ratweek*), played havoc and demoralized the Germans and their auxiliary allies. As a result, SS-Geb.Pi.Btl. 13 of the Handschar took part in repairing 18 kilometers of railway track that transported the invaluable bauxite, wrecked in one night by the partisans.

September 1944 was marked by massive desertions among the Muslim volunteers (called "Croats") of all ranks, vanishing with arms and equipment, in fear of seeing the Germans abandoning their country, following rumors circulating among the troops. Occasionally their German officers simply "disappeared." The Kama, still in the process of being formed, suffered from this problem and the imams were asked to intervene. The critical situation for all German forces, the after effects of Operation *Bagration,* and the Allied landings in France, could no longer be hidden.

1.GD was deployed to the east of Nič to establish a buffer and absorb Army Group South Ukraine now facing Bulgaria.

Tito indeed was trying to regroup his forces—two corps in the Gornji–Milanovac–Lazarevac–Valjevo region—to take Belgrade, the future capital of his popular republic. On

September 24, Otto Kumm was ordered to destroy them by using those German forces under his command already in contact. On the 25th, his own regiments set off and established contact in turn. But, on the 26th, Kumm received top-secret orders: Red Army vanguards had gone through the Iron Gates on the Danube, and the division was to relieve 1.GD in the Nič region, leaving a reinforced regiment (SS-GJR14) in the sector, so that 1.GD could contain this breakthrough and give Army Group E time to counterattack, with a maximum of resources, toward the Bulgarian frontier. A particularly complex crisis situation developed on September 29, 1944, and the situation in the south of Hungary and the northern Balkans had to be taken into consideration (see chapter "The Balkans, and Crete, 1941" in *German Mountain Troops 1939–42*).

While it was advancing, the Prinz Eugen was attacked by Titoists, Chetniks, and a Bulgarian vanguard, who were aware that the Soviets were reinforcing their positions less than 100 kilometers from Belgrade, and who had also crossed the Bulgarian border in front of 1.GD whose supply lines they were threatening. On their side, Handschar bases were attacked in the east of Bosnia, to the south of the River Jania, especially after October 3. IX. Waffen-Gebirgs-Korps der SS (Kroatisches) reached Andrijasevci, five kilometers to the southwest of Vinkovici on October 3. The Kama units, who were operationally sound, were committed to the fight at Bácska on the 9th under command of Colonel Lombard.

On October 3, 1944, Hitler ordered the Balkans to be evacuated. The units mentioned above were given the major task and headache of keeping a passage open for Germans retreating northward, despite the Soviet breakthroughs supported by partisans. Among his other strategic and political objectives, the Führer wanted to protect his Croatian ally.

The Prinz Eugen managed to arrive east of Nič, relieve 1.GD, and position itself as a buffer between Zajecar and the Leskovac, on October 6, after absorbing local units with little operational value and hundreds of wounded that rear echelons were unable to evacuate, either by land or air.

Given the enemy position, annihilation appeared the only possible outcome for the division. Indeed, Armeekorps Müller assessed the situation as follows: to the east was the 2nd Bulgarian Army (with seven national divisions and three Soviet ones), and the 57th Soviet Army with one armored corps and nine divisions of fusiliers, and behind that, seven partisan divisions.

With the Prinz Eugen's strongpoints outflanked and its mobile reserve engaged, the division ended up falling back on successive defensive lines, mostly away from the roads, by night and by day, in territory infested with partisans, and with the Soviet and Bulgarian columns at its heels: ironically, the Bulgarians were equipped with German armor, aircraft, and automatic weapons. Without any logistics support, crossing the Jastrebac Heights and the Kopaonik Mountains, the division was pushed to the limits of its capacity to resist; indeed, Bulgarian

In the Prinz Eugen (but also in "Nord"), and not seen in other units, were special hobnailed *Bergschuhen* with the tip of the toe raised, like Finnish boots. General Phleps himself wore them. Some had steel attachments so they could be worn with skis. (Private collection)

It is unclear whether these riders belong to the Prinz Eugen, as the features were the same from one division to another; this photo from *Signal* enables us to appreciate the specific equipment of these reconnaissance battalions. Wearing hobnailed *Bergschuhen* was incompatible with riding horses.

national radio announced it had been annihilated. Several units and their command posts were captured with no prisoners spared. The division was finally recovered by Army Group E on the Novi Pazar–Kraljevo defensive line. The division positioned itself around the town with less than 4,000 troops, in a bridgehead at the confluence of the Ibar and Morava rivers. After they'd entered Nič on the 15th, having crossing the Morava, the Soviets reached these new positions on October 22.

The Handschar managed to stabilize its operational area with the bridgehead at Brcko and destroy an enemy column. But its lack of means led Hample to ask that the unit be withdrawn from the front. Leaving reinforced SS-GJR28 on the Save under 1.GD which had just arrived from Serbia, the division began its withdrawal to the north of Croatia and Zagreb (Agram) on October 16, 1944. Although it sustained no losses from enemy action, it suffered from the persistent mass desertions of Bosnians, who now realized that they would never return to the country they had committed themselves to defending. *Volkdeutsche* and Muslims joined their columns, together with pressganged recruits.

As a final act in this debacle, Kama mutinied on October 17 and was formally disbanded on the 31st. A few "faithfuls" managed to reach Handschar whose entire divisional HQ security company deserted on the 21st, incited to do so by its imam, Abdullah Muhasilovic; it went over to the partisans.

The Prinz Eugen pursued the Titoists in Bosnia-Herzegovina in the summer of 1943, "cleansing" local villages one after the other. (DR)

Allied support for the partisans was manifest in 1943: these *Gebirgsjäger* have discovered containers of arms including Sten guns.

XI.AK positioned itself in Zagreb. On October 20 1944, Tito's partisans liberated Belgrade and welcomed in the Soviet troops. On October 24, horrified by the situation with the "Croat" units in Waffen-SS uniform (Muslims mostly), Himmler ordered Sauberzweig to disarm them and pick out and assemble the loyalists in Kampfgruppen Handschar and Hanke under 1.GD. Operation *Herbstlaub* (*Autumn Leaves*) started on the 25th at Brčko and lasted several days with no major incidents. A number of the volunteers became *Hiwis* in 1.GD. Pressure from the enemy tailed off and few incidents marked October. However, in November Handschar remnants were frequently attacked by the partisans east of Zagreb.

In these fragile circumstances, Kampfgruppe Hanke, which had incorporated several Handschar remnants, was ordered on November 9, 1944 to position itself in a final defensive line at Apatin, in Hungary, on the other side of the Drave, under command of LXVIII.AK. The "Muslim Division" left the Balkans and its dreams of independence once and for all, for the Eastern Front. 1.GD reached the southern end of Lake Balaton, facing east. During November, the Prinz Eugen kept the routes open for the withdrawal of the army group and held the bridgehead at Kraljevo until the 28th when the last unit passed through. after destroying any infrastructure that would slow the Red Army advance: bridges, aerodromes, stations, roads, and railways. This resistance saved Army Group E and earned the divisional commander, Otto Kumm, the swords to his Knight's Cross with oak leaves.

On November 11, 1944, Veles, then Skopje during the night of 13th/14th, were both abandoned. Localized counterattacks enabled the retreating units to get through and maintain the cohesion of the defensive positions. Besides, until February 1945, V.SS-Gebirgs-Armee-Korps, behind the withdrawing German forces, continued its anti-partisan operations, mainly in Bosnia-Herzegovina. The Corps HQ and several organic units transferred to the Eastern Front in the center under command of 9. Armee. Its mission was to hold the Frankfurt an der Oder sector. It ended the war in May 1945 in the Berlin region.

Wearing period dress is a reenactment soldier from the Handschar: *Feldgrau* fez, M42 twill jacket, M42 shirt and trousers with the Reischwehr *Abzeichentuch* (literally badge cloth) oversleeves, "Styrian" gaiters, *Bergschuhe*, and weaponry including a *Schießbecher* (grenade launcher) with anti-personnel grenade ready for use. (Private collection)

This colorized image is of a radio team from the Albanian Battalion of the Handschar, recognizable by the conic fez pinched at the top. The operator wearing a *Bergmütze* is German, as were most personnel in positions of command. (National Contemporary History Museum, Ljubljana)

Greece

The Resistance in Italian-controlled Greece was quick to flourish. One action deserves a special mention for its strategic effect: destroying the railway bridge over the Gorgopotamos on October 25, 1942, by Andartes and British commandos (Operation *Harling*). The resulting effect was that, apart from its obvious local impact, it seriously disrupted German logistics. This bridge on the only railway line to Piraeus was strategically very important: supplying the DAK was interrupted for six weeks during a key period (the launching of the second battle of El Alamein) and contributed to forcing Rommel's withdrawal (see the earlier chapter "North Africa, 1942–43"). When, on May 13, 1943, Panzerarmee Afrika capitulated, Hitler was busy with the next stage of the war and how the second front that Stalin wanted would open.

The southern flank of "Fortress Europe" could indeed be threatened in France, in Italy, and in the Balkans. In order to force the Germans to strengthen this region by removing their units from Sicily, the British launched Operation *Mincemeat*. In an adjunct to Operation *Husky* (the invasion of the island), a major operation, *Animals*, was launched by the Greek Resistance (destroying the major viaduct across the Achelos) on July 2, intended to divert OKW's attention from Sicily.

Greek Resistance was divided into two factions: the National Republican Greek League (EDES), the monarchists, commanded by Napoleon Zervas, to the west of the River Arachthos, and the Greek People's Liberation Army (ELAS), the Communists, under Aris Velouchiotis, to the east of the river. The most difficult area for the Italians was the Pindhos range and the neighboring mountains. The 9th Armata's C.-in-C., whose command post was in Albania, thought that all Greek men were potential partisans and that pacifying the country required all the males in the country to be arrested, which the Italian command in Athens refused to countenance.

The fear of an Allied landing on the western coast of Greece to the north of Patras meant that XXII. Geb.-AK under Lieutenant General

Artillerymen from SS-GAR13 serving a 10.5cm Gebirgshaubitze 40 (mountain howitzer), probably during training, as the wheels have been removed. The gun commander on the left is an NCO.

This *SS-Hauptsturmführer* (captain) from the Handschar chats with two volunteers. They are all wearing a camouflaged smock; the officer is wearing his rank on the collar and on the sleeve. (Colorization. DR)

Hubert Lanz—who had only arrived on September 9—was put on alert. Brought out of the Kuban bridgehead in March 1943, 1.GD—under Major General Walter von Stettner Ritter von Grabenhofen, who had commanded the unit since January 1—joined the army corps to constitute its kernel later in April after a period for refitting and reforming in Montenegro. When it arrived at Nič between April 4–18, 1.GD first took part in Operation *Schwarz* (the fifth anti-partisan offensive) from mid-May to mid-June, in the west of Montenegro. On June 19, it set off for the north of Greece (Florina). At the end of the month, it reached the Ioannina–Arta sector, in Epirus, along the Pindhos range, near the Albanian border.

On June 30, 1943, Kampfgruppe Salminger, regrouping to the south of Kozani, was given the task keeping the Servia–Elasson corridor open: getting bridges operational again, occupying the passes, and helping to keep the convoys moving.

By July 3, the mission, dealing with groups of Graeco-Albanian partisans, had been accomplished. On July 7, 1943, on orders from its new commander, Lieutenant Colonel Pfeiffer, a former 1.GD veteran, 2. Regiment Brandenburg[3]—the bearer of the *Gebirgstruppen* traditions—had moved to Greece, to Ptolemais so as to secure the Thessalonika–Athens railway line. The region had been "cleansed" by the Geheime Feldpolizei at the end of April. The unit discovered how taxing anti-partisan operations were, alongside Wehrmacht, Waffen-SS, and Polizei units, as well as their local auxiliaries. 2. Regiment Brandenburg took part in disarming their former Italian ally in September. It fought in the north of Greece (Florina) and in Albania (Tirana, Korca), then in Montenegro (Skopje, Raška), and in the east of Bosnia, until September 18.

On July 7, 1943, von Stettner addressed his troops with these orders: "All localities that can offer shelter to the [partisan] bands must be destroyed, the men must be either shot if they are suspected of participating in the fighting and supporting the *Banden*, or arrested at once and imprisoned."

3 On April 1, 1943, Sonderverband Brandenburg became Division Brandenburg with four regiments, including 2. Regiment Brandenburg, with three battalions under command of Lieutenant Colonel von Kobelinsky, derived from II. Bataillon, which had a "mountain" calling. Its headquarters were at Baden, to the south of Vienna, then at Admont in the Tyrol. The new I./2.Rgt. Brandenburg was commanded by Captain Weithoener, II. by Captain Oesterwitz, and III. by Captain Renner. A signals company and, from 1944 onward, a mountain artillery battery with four guns constituted the regimental organic units. 4.Regiment B. was already engaged in this theater, notably for the fifth operation.

Before receiving Sturmgeschütze IIIs, Prinz Eugen, at the insistent request of Phleps, was equipped with captured French tanks, like this Renault B1-bis. Placed under command of Captain Harry Paletta, this unit saved the Prinz Eugen subunits on more than one occasion. The crew wear the Panzer-black uniform with the Odal rune on the collar, but without the edelweiss.

These instructions summarized a good part of German policy concerning counter-guerilla activity. OB Army Goup E (*Generaloberst der Luftwaffe* Alexander Löhr) at von Stettner's request, gave the regimental COs carte blanche to arrest anyone bearing arms or near a *Band* and to carry out *Sühnemaßnahmen*, or "expiatory measures."

On July 25, 1943, Mussolini's arrest led the German command to think twice about entrusting security missions to Italians when Operation *Achse* was launched. In the end, a minimal occupation was accepted, limited to the larger towns and major routes, in certain regions of Greece. But the Germans began monitoring Italian communications very closely, interpreting orders given by the Italian authorities and determining their intentions.

A Handschar *Jäger* wearing a cloth field jacket. (DR)

GJR98 (Lieutenant Colonel Josef Salminger) in 1.GD, using this situation assessment, was ordered therefore to "cleanse" the main Ionnina–Preveza road via the Gulf of Arta, whilst still being capable of reacting to an Allied landing. The regimental commander had a very ideological approach to his mission and considered his unit as *Hitler'sches Regiment*. Wounded 14 times, he was a hard man but adored by his *Jäger* and particularly appreciated by Lanz. He directed Operation *Salminger* from July 22–26, 1943. In July alone, 20 or so villages were destroyed along the roads. He attacked and "cleansed" the village of Moutsiotitas, killing more than 150 people, including women, children, and the elderly. On August 16, the same thing happened in the village of Kommeno, with 317 killed,[4] including a priest and all the guests at a wedding, massacred by 12.Kp. (First Lieutenant Willy Röser) from III./GJR98 (Major Reinhold Klebe) using mortars, grenades, and finally light arms. There

---

4 172 women, 145 men, 97 children under 15, 13 babies, 14 old people; 38 were burned in their houses; 181 dwellings were destroyed.

Lieutenant General Hubert Lanz commanded XXII. Geb.-AK at Ioannina in Greece. (DR alirafikkhan)

was no response, indicating that partisans were not present in the area at the time, but two groups (ELAS and EDES) had been observed a few days previously by Salminger himself. Several *Jäger*, including a platoon leader, refused to carry out the orders and the company commander was jeered.

Official reports concealed the facts at every level: it was claimed that return fire came from the village, which Greek survivors and German witnesses were able to contradict and denounce the excesses of murderous madness, if not sadism, carried out nonstop for five hours. From an operational perspective, German reports qualified these operations as futile, since the partisans (Andartes) had camouflaged their weapons and transformed themselves into peaceful peasants.

After remarks made to the Italian authorities, von Stettner made inquiries and withdrew Röser's and Salminger's commands. The latter was succeeded by Major Harald von Hirschfeld. The departure of the GJR98 commander was celebrated at a farewell party at the corps command at Ionnina. After leaving the festivities, Salminger's vehicle ran into a telegraph pole placed across the road by EDES partisans and he was killed outright.

On October 1, 1943, after "settling" the disarmament of the Italians, General Lanz ordered that the death of Salminger be avenged by launching pitiless reprisal operations. More than 200 civilians were executed, a dozen villages were burned, in particular Lingiades, where Kampfgruppe Dodel liquidated 87 civilians on October 3 "to set an example."

In September 1943, after Italy—the principal occupation force in Greece—switched sides, 1.GD disarmed its former allies.

And then the worst happened. After a battalion of GJR99, transported by barge and by the Luftwaffe, had been driven off by artillery fire on September 10, Kampfgruppe von Hirschfeld with four companies from GJR98, a battalion from 104.JgD, and artillery and

A column of dispatch riders waiting behind the Stab 1.GD command vehicles. They are wearing protective coats made of green oilskin or khaki heavy twill cloth. (Franz Moll Archives)

engineer elements were indeed dispatched to the island of Kefalonia on the 19th to disarm elements of the Italian 33rd Infantry Division Acqui who tried to resist, with shots fired.

The outcome was that the Germans executed 4,000 Italian soldiers in cold blood, then left the scene singing. On the 23rd, the same happened on the island of Corfu. Von Hirschfeld and Klebe were identified as responsible for these massacres after the war. The former fell in combat in East Prussia in 1945; the latter survived and contributed to the reforming of 1.GD in the Bundeswehr. Röser was killed during an air raid on Freiburg in 1944, and Dodel and von Stettner while falling back from the Balkans toward the Reich in 1944. Lanz, tried for war crimes after the war, was sentenced to 12 years in prison but only served three. 1./GJB54 also assassinated Italian officers in Albania without trial.

At the beginning of 1943, 1.GD was sent to Florina, in northern Greece before continuing toward Kosovo, Mitrovica, and Novi Pazar, from where it prepared its offensive into Bosnia on December 4, 1943 (see Operation *Kugelblitz*). In order to reinforce its anti-partisan elements by drawing support from mountain warfare specialists and by anticipating Italy's defection, the high command had SS-Pol.GJR18 recalled to the Balkans after eight months on the Karelia Front. Indeed, on August 2, 1943, the regiment left the northern front and, on the 15th, its first elements were assembled in Greece, at Lianikladion, near Larissa.

III. Bataillon was engaged immediately alongside some Brandenburger and the 11. Luftwaffen-Felddivision as coastal defense to the southeast of Athens. Between September 17–23, it embarked aboard anti-submarine Flotilla 21 and the Attica coastal defense flotilla to disarm an Italian division on the island of Eubea and in the Cyclades. With naval artillery support, the only operation that experienced any significant Italian resistance was at Andros. British resistance on Leyitha, near Turkey, also collapsed. The battalion guarded these islands for three months until December 26, 1943.

I./SS-Pol.GJR18 moved to Corinth at the beginning of November. With its I. and II. Bataillone, the regiment took part in securing the Lamia–Athens axes in December. The regiment then took part in anti-partisan operations: in the Taygetos Mountains (II. and III./SS-Pol.GJR 18 as well as the artillery battalion) from June 6–21, 1944, and Operation *Kreuzotter* (*Adder*) in the Parnon Hills near Amfissa, from August 5–25, 1944, with the same units; at the same time, I./SS-Pol.GJR 18 was engaged in the Thessalonica region. As a unit of the Ordnungspolizei, this latter regiment rounded up about 1,700 Jews in Athens and deported them to Auschwitz, with its personnel reportedly accompanying the trains.

At the end of June, Lieutenant Colonel Salminger (commander GJR98) arrives with his *Kampgruppe* to the south of Kozani. (Franz Moll Archives)

These men from the Stab 1.GD are wearing *Feldgrau* wool cloth or M42 canvas cloth uniforms. The *Oberfeldwebel* (master sergeant) in *Feldgrau* is holding a *Tropenmütze*. The red canvas lining could be used for sending optical signals. (Franz Moll Archives)

1.GD did the same with 2,000 Jews taken in the Ionnina region in March 1944. In August, mountain police assisted in arresting Communists in Athens, supporting the Greek police.

In September 1944, the withdrawal north began. III. Bataillon was ambushed at Toppola. The partisans had adopted horseshoe positions into which the battalion entered without realizing. The trap closed in on the column's rear and the slaughter began. The only survivors were one officer and 11 mountain policemen.

At the beginning of May 1944, 1.GD as a *Feuerwehr* (fire brigade) in southeastern Europe returned to Yugoslavia once again by train, disembarking to the north of Belgrade: the railway line to Greece had been destroyed by Allied aircraft and the bridges over the Danube were continually being attacked. Then via Macedonia by land, it reached Epirus, the Ioannina region, the Adriatic coast, and the Albanian border. From May 3 to July 20, 1944, it carried out small-scale operations against partisans, at Metsovon and Argyrokastron, in the Pindhos range and in the south of Albania. The unfolding Yugoslav situation caused the German command to deploy 1.GD to Montenegro and from there to Serbia. Its lead elements reached Mitrovica on July 25.

Clashes broke out between ELAS and EDES in October/November 1944, which resulted in leaders being targeted and murdered, with attempts to "instrumentalize" the Germans with a view to preparing the postwar period.

A column of vehicles regroups at a dangerous section of road, as the signpost on the right indicates: movement forbidden to all vehicles traveling alone, minimum five trucks, weapons ready for action, danger of mines, road closed from 1800 to 0500, indicating there were active partisans in this area.

Artillerymen from GAR79 remove gun parts from their transport, in order to assemble the artillery piece. (ECPAD)

Securing supply routes was a constant preoccupation, in particular bridges, like this one guarded on all sides.

Polizei-Gebirgsjäger-Regiment 18 during an anti-partisan operation: its artillery battalion advances through snow (above); tankers with *grünmeliert* heavy cloth overalls in discussion (left); and faces etched by the intensity of the fighting (below). (Poys Archives)

Summer dress for the SS-Pol.-GJR18 worn in Greece: *Polizei-Tropenmütze* with an Army-edelweiss on the left side, saharan shirt and shorts (from Waffen-SS depots) and *Bergschuhe*. (Private collection)

Another major unit using the appellation "*Gebirgs*" was engaged in Greece: XXII. Geb.-AK was constituted in August 1943. From September 1943 to March 1944, it oversaw anti-partisan operations in Greece. In April 1944, it took part in Operation *Margarethe*, keeping Hungary within the Axis. In November 1944, it left Greece for the Veles region in center of Macedonia, where it absorbed several infantry units that had been guarding lines of communications before reaching Hungary and the Lake Balaton region in December. It finished the war in Carinthia and Styria.

Albania

Resistance networks flourished in Albania, occupied by Italy since 1940. Italy's defection naturally changed things.

In September 1943, First Lieutenant Lange, a mountain Brandenburger, and one of the few survivors from the battalion of Caucasian volunteers he had commanded during Operation *Schamil* in the Caucasus, a stinging failure (see earlier chapter "The Eastern Front, 1942–45"), took charge of the Albanian militia from the anti-communist, anti-Italian, anti-royalist Balli Kombetar resistance movement in the Tirana region, in order to relieve German units. These counterinsurgency forces, armed with captured Italian equipment, fought against the *Banden* and their British instructors from the end of 1943 to June 1944 in the Shkodar and Prizren regions. Although 21. SS-Gebirgs-Division Skanderbeg was referred to as Albanian, it was mostly recruited from among the Muslim Albanian-speaking Kosovars from Kosovo.

It was mainly stationed in the Skopje–Kumanovo–Presevo–Bujanovac region during its brief operational existence. It was commanded from April to June 1944 during its initial

operations in Montenegro by Major General Josef Fitshum, then by Colonel August Schmidhuber. The second Albanian unit proposed by Sauberzweig never saw the light of day. Skanderbeg operated in southern Serbia and in Kosovo-Metochia, especially around Pec, Gnjilzne, Djakovica, Tetovo Gostivar, and Kosovska Mitrovica.

This II./GJR98 *Ullr* commemorates the unit's passage through the Balkans in 1943/4. (Private collection)

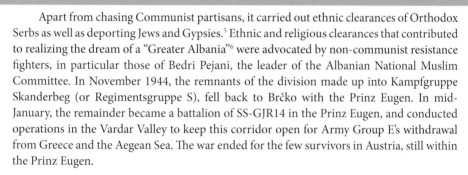

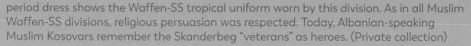

Skanderbeg

Insignia specific to the Skanderbeg Division: escutcheons worn on the *Feldbluse*, cuff band and conical fez. (Private collections)

In April 1944, it was decided to raise a new Muslim division, 21. Waffen-Gebirgs-Division der SS Skanderbeg, recruited from Albanian-speaking Kosovars. This reenactment in period dress shows the Waffen-SS tropical uniform worn by this division. As in all Muslim Waffen-SS divisions, religious persuasion was respected. Today, Albanian-speaking Muslim Kosovars remember the Skanderbeg "veterans" as heroes. (Private collection)

The Balkans, 1942–45

Apart from chasing Communist partisans, it carried out ethnic clearances of Orthodox Serbs as well as deporting Jews and Gypsies.[5] Ethnic and religious clearances that contributed to realizing the dream of a "Greater Albania"[6] were advocated by non-communist resistance fighters, in particular those of Bedri Pejani, the leader of the Albanian National Muslim Committee. In November 1944, the remnants of the division made up into Kampfgruppe Skanderbeg (or Regimentsgruppe S), fell back to Brčko with the Prinz Eugen. In mid-January, the remainder became a battalion of SS-GJR14 in the Prinz Eugen, and conducted operations in the Vardar Valley to keep this corridor open for Army Group E's withdrawal from Greece and the Aegean Sea. The war ended for the few survivors in Austria, still within the Prinz Eugen.

XXI.Geb.AK, constituted in September 1943, carried out anti-partisan operations in Serbia then in Croatia without using any mountain units. On September 11, 1944, OB Südost assigned the corps to Army Group E. In October 1944, it had to withdraw from Bosnia to the Tirana region, leaving Albania on the 17th. During November and December, it continued its retreat north, along a limited number of routes in bad condition, harassed by aggressive partisans along the way, targeting the columns of soft-skinned vehicles. Nevertheless 22,000 troops managed to evade capture and almost certain death. XXI.Geb.AK was operational in the Sokolac–Vlasenica region in January 1945 then to the north of the Save in April.

Falling Back on Reich Territory

The Romanian and Bulgarian defections in the fall of 1944 left the gates to Yugoslavia wide open for the Red Army. The difficult terrain, which the mountain units mastered, turned out to be hell for other units from the Heer, the Waffen-SS, the Luftwaffe, the Kriegsmarine,

---

5 The genocide in Bosnia-Herzegovina is estimated at 200,000 Serbs, almost 22,000 Jews (out of 24,000) and thousands of Gypsies. The Muslim Waffen-SS units left a bloody trail behind them, with "technical purification"—only destroying the villages, including homes, to force people to leave—being denied them.

6 Regrouping Kosovo-Metochia, the west of Macedonia, the south of Montenegro, Bosnia-Herzegovina, and the Sandžak into a great pan-Islamic state in the Balkans. This project was put to the Grand Mufti of Jerusalem, Hadj Amin el Husseini, who approved it, but ultimately the Germans overruled the idea.

Major Oesterwitz took command of 2. Regiment Brandenburg. He is wearing the proper cuff band and the edelweiss on the sleeve and *Bergmütze*.

and the territorial services, who were often unfit for combat and unable to cover long distances. On September 6, 1944, the order to evacuate the Balkans was given. The Soviets had reached the Danube and were threatening to encircle the entire OB Südost, around Belgrade, Fiume, and the Adriatic. Tito wanted to liberate Belgrade with his own troops, with the help of the Soviets if necessary, to liberate the capital of his future people's republic.

The assault on Belgrade itself began on October 14, 1944. Thanks to Soviet air support, the 3rd Ukrainian Front and the Yugoslav Army of Liberation penetrated the city. Tito had his capital. The Germans were encircled between Belgrade and Smlederevo on the 20th. On the 24th, Belgrade and its environs were declared secure after bitter fighting on the Danube and for control of Pančevo and Kraljevo. Withdrawal northwest over the Save was inevitable.

2. Regiment Brandenburg suffered the same fate as the other units in this sector, in particular 1.GD. The regiment held its positions in Hungary on the banks of Lake Balaton, but the Brandenburgers ended up by being exfiltrated from this front and were transformed into a panzergrenadier division as planned, in East Prussia. In the main, mountain deployments stopped. The edelweiss was sometimes still worn, fidelity to the *Gebirgstruppen* being obligatory. II. Gebirgsjäger-Bataillon, stationed at Baden then at Veldens in Carinthia was the depot for 2. Regiment Brandenburg which was included in a *Lehrregiment* (a depot and instruction regiment) and became Gebirgs-Grundausbildungs-Bataillon (elementary mountain instruction regiment).

Between September 2–23, before falling back in mid-October to the south of Belgrade through Pogarevac, 1.GD had been relieved by part of the Prinz Eugen, also withdrawing west, after heavy fighting between Vlasotin and Zajecar, along the Bulgaro-Yugoslav border, to the southeast of Serbia and to the northeast of Nič.

On October 17, von Stettner gave up the idea of breaking through toward Belgrade and decided to continue falling back west. Only part of the division reached the Drina, with 5,000 troops left behind in the Belgrade *Kessel* (cauldron), where they were captured and the divisional commander killed. Before the end of the month, Lieutenant General August Wittmann took command of 1.GD's remnants and set them up defensively in the triangle formed by the confluence of the Drina and the Save. After isolated operations, the division was engaged south of Lake Balaton. General Josef Kübler then took over command on December 17, 1944. Winter slowed down operations and gave the unit time to refurbish.

I. and II./SS-Pol.-GJR18 took part in the battle of Belgrade in October. The commander, *Major der Schutzpolizei* Mann, was killed by a mine and Major Johann Poys succeeded him. On October 23, the regiment positioned itself defensively on Novo Pasovo, as part of Kampfgruppe Zirngibel from Division Böttcher, a mixture of units under Lieutenant General Karl Böttcher, made up into *Kampfgruppen* and placed under command of 2. Panzerarmee's Höherer Artillerie-Kommandeur 305 (Artillery High Command). The lack of Soviet pressure enabled the Germans to fall back on Irig, in Voyvodina (Syrmia) and position themselves in an area infested with partisans, active in the Fruska Gora Mountains.

The division's reaction reserve consisted of SS-Pz.Jäg.Abt.7 from the Prinz Eugen, with Sturmgeschützgruppe Paletta (SS-Sturmgeschütz-Abteilung 105 in V.SS-Geb.AK) in particular and its nine StuGs facing 300 Soviet tanks. In the evening of October 25, a Soviet attack forced the unit back into the second echelon, despite the intervention of its own tanks, and on the 26th it found itself involved in anti-partisan operations northwest of the Fruska Gora.

Böttcher reproached Major Poys for having retreated from his position, saying that he'd had a regimental commander shot for doing the same thing. The major explained that withdrawal had saved his unit from capture and that therefore it was still operational. SS-Pol.-GJR18 left Division Böttcher and joined its immediate neighbor, General Kübler's *Korpsgruppe*, ensuring liaison with Kampfgruppe Zirngibel from October 27–31, before positioning itself in the Mandelos region on November 1. The police *Jäger* were exhausted, their uniforms in tatters—some were still wearing tropical gear issued in Greece that offered no protection whatsoever against the humid cold of the Syrmian fall—and with no illusions as to the fate of the German armies who, for weeks on end now, had become used to accomplishing the impossible.

They continued to slowly withdraw west, marked by fighting at Basenova, Mandelos, Kusmin, and Osijek from November 1944 to February 1945, Valpovo and Noskovski in February and March 1945, Vasala and Varazdin in April, Koprivnica at the end of April/early May, and Ludberg/Jadzabet in Croatia on May 8/9, 1945. During this last period, what was left of the regiment was used as a rearguard for the XV. Kosaken-Kavallerie-Korps under Lieutenant General Helmuth von Pannwitz trying to avoid capture by the Russians[7] to whom the mountain police surrendered.

Out of its 4,800 men, SS-Pol.-GJR18 lost 3,080 killed, wounded or missing in three years of almost continuous fighting. After leaving Kraljevo, the Prinz Eugen fell back on Cacak, with the Soviets at its heels, then on Ljubovija.

Regimentsgruppe Skanderbeg under Lieutenant Colonel Graf joined the division together with some Kriegsmarine personnel. The division, within XXXIV.AK's structure, fell back on Brčko via Rogacica, Ljubovija, Zvornik, Losnica, and Bijeljina, then toward Vinkovici and Vukovar. Most of Army Group E headed for Sarajevo. During this withdrawal, the Prinz Eugen was given the task of keeping the corridors open on the Drina.

---

7 The Cossacks were unaware of the agreement among the Allies which stipulated that any of their nationals caught serving in German uniform were to be handed over back to their country of origin. The British therefore handed them over to the Soviets at Linz and few survived.

The M40 dress shows off its camouflage qualities. This uniform was issued to all Waffen-SS divisions in the Balkans. (Private collection)

A surprising period of calm in early December 1944 allowed the division to restore some of its strength with young recruits and improved officer training. After December 20, however, pressure from Titoist partisans and Chetniks, supported by artillery and Soviet Katyushas, resumed, reaching a peak at Christmas. The regiments found themselves once again fighting anywhere and everywhere.

At the start of 1945 1.GD, successively under command of LXVIII.AK (Konrad) and XXII.AK (Lanz) took part in one of the last decisive battles of the war, in the marshes south of Lake Balaton, the linchpin to the Gross Reich.

On March 12, 1945, 1.GD became 1. Volks-Gebirgs-Division (VGD), the only mountain unit to have been given the appellation *Volks*, or People's. During the last two weeks of March, Wittmann resumed command of 1.GD. Backed onto a defensive line, at the junction of the provinces of Styria and Burgenland (eastern Austria), and the Hochwechsel Mountains, he succeeded in stopping the Soviet breakthrough toward Styria.

A new division, 9.GD (Ost),[8] made up of *Gebirgstruppen* schools and various other support and rear-echelon units of the Heer, the Waffen-SS, and the Luftwaffe stationed in Styria, was engaged on 1.GD's left, in the Semmering region. This initiative—aimed at ensuring a coherent front between 6.PzArmee and 6. Armee by dovetailing the two armies—came from *General der Gebirgstruppen* Julius Ringel, already mentioned several times as *Befehlshaber* (commander) of Wehrkreis XVIII (Gebirgs-Wehrkreis). It was called in turn Korpsgruppe Semmering, Gruppe Semmering, Kampfgruppe Raithel, Kampfgruppe Semmering, and, finally, designated 9.GD on May 1, 1945.

The units gradually arrived in the operational area, a line west and south of Gloggnitz: GJR154 and GJR155,[9] GAR56 (two mountain howitzer battalions), Geb-A.A.56, Pz.Jg-E&A-Kp48, and one *Geb.-Pi.Kp.* Under Colonel Heribert Raithel, 9.GD only had a few weeks in which to prove itself before hostilities ceased: on April 17, the Soviet forces in Styria were driven back following the intervention of 1.VGD, 1.PzD, and 117.JgD in the sector. Fighting took place mainly at company level, with Soviet forces that vastly outnumbered the Germans; losses were heavy among these *Alarmeinheiten* (emergency units) whose personnel was usually unfit for combat in the field.

---

8 See the "Norway and Finland, 1942–45" chapter for comments on Div.-Gruppe Kräutler which had become 9.GD (Nord).
9 III./GJR155 was mainly made up of personnel from the Luftwaffe (JG27), the Waffen-SS (SS-GJ-E&A-Btl 13), the Handschar's depot battalion, and the Nordland Division's depot company.

Final awards were presented on the 1.GD front on April 14, 1945. Here, Lieutenant General Josef Kübler has just awarded the Knight's Cross to Sergeant Georg Audenrieth (I./GJR99). (Audenrieth Archives)

Despite losses, the mission had been accomplished: 6. Armee was not taken from behind. Several 9.GD soldiers were shot for deserting and undermining morale by 6. Armee's mobile martial court. The Germans left the Balkans. With the conflict in Yugoslavia coming to an end, the Syrmian Front was established, a line of defense relying on the fortifications in Syrmia and to the east of Slavonia. At the beginning of January, the Prinz Eugen, still reinforced by the Regimentsgruppe Skanderbeg (and its StuG battery), took the initiative in the Otok–Novo Selo sector by destroying a dense concentration of antitank weapons, then, having secured its sector, it fell back on the Vrbanja–Gradiste–Vinkovici region, leaving Rgt.-Gr. Skanderbeg as a rearguard.

On January 17, 1945, XXIV.AK (*General der Flieger* Hellmuth Felmy of the Luftwaffe, a former commander of the Orientkorps) launched a counterattack—Operation *Frühlingssturm* (*Spring Storm*)—on the Syrmian Front, in order to relieve the pressure on 2.Pz.Armee to the north of the Danube. The Prinz Eugen attacked on the corps' axis, along the Danube. The ground was retaken in two days and enabled new positions to be established which were held until the spring.

Otto Kumm took command of 1. SS-Panzer-Division Leibstandarte Adolf Hitler and *SS-Brigadeführer* August Schmiduber took over the Prinz Eugen. Skanderbeg, now reduced to a battalion having lost its sailors, became II./SS-GJR14. With the help of their Soviet and Bulgarian allies, the Yugoslav partisans (including some Italians) had a difficult winter campaign on the Syrmian Front—13,000 partisans, 1,100 Soviets and 630 Bulgarian soldiers killed, for 30,000 Germans deaths—before breaking through on April 12, 1945, marking the end of the liberation of Yugoslavia. According to the historian Srdan Cvetkovic, instead of executing them during the Communist purges in Serbia in 1944/5, the partisans forced collaborators and "enemies of the people" to fight on the frontlines.

Vienna was under threat during the winter of 1944/5. Backing on holding the Lake Balaton–Danube–Drave triangle, Army Group South studied the possibility of a vast operation to retake Budapest, in Operation *Wehrwolf*. For this operation, the Prinz Eugen was subordinated to XCI.AK, operations lasting from February 4–25, 1945, between Našice and Virovitica in the Papuk Mountains. On March 1, the division was transported, partly by rail, to the north of Zenica—the steel factories were still working—where it was subordinated to XXI.Geb.-AK. From the outskirts of Sarajevo (Illidza), it attacked south, towards Trnovo (a gully at the bottom of the Sarajevo basin) by the gorges and the plateau of Kalinovik, then

As an amalgamation of marching battalions engaged in the Semmering region under command of Colonel Heribert Raithel, 9.GD Ost wore a range of Wehrmacht and Waffen-SS uniforms. One item that was worn by the SS-Gebirgsjäger-Ersatz-Bataillon Leoben was the Italian camouflage heavy cloth version of the fur-lined parka worn by the Waffen-SS. (Private collection)

Foca, in order to disengage 181.ID, in great difficulty with partisans between Goražde and Foca, on the banks of the Drina.

This division—which included III./Sonderverband Bergmann (see the chapter "The Eastern Front, 1941–42" in *German Mountain Troops 1939–42*)—was once again encircled to the east of Sarajevo a few days later and had to be extricated by the Prinz Eugen. On April 17, the Prinz Eugen fell back on Doboj and continued toward the Save, level with Brod where heavy fighting had broken out. It crossed to the north of the river, ensuring the rear of XXXIV.AK, to which it was transferred in late April, toward Zagreb (Agram). As reserve for Army Group E on April 29, then detached to XCI.AK, the division was engaged to the west of Zagreb then Karlovac, from where it tried to break through to the southwest on May 6.

The announcement of the capitulation on May 8 decided XCI.AK would move peacefully to Austria, which was impossible given the harassment by partisans who did not respect the terms of the armistice. The division ensured the rest of the corps could withdraw, only surrendering the heavy weapons on May 11. Having been relieved of their oath, a few *Jäger*, singly or in small groups, succeeded in making their way to Austria. But the unavoidable unconditional surrender was fast approaching. After laying down their arms, 150,000 troops were marched off into captivity. Thousands were liquidated, the campaign in the Balkans having left a trail of blood that needed vengeance. It was thus, on May 14/15,

1945 when Germany had already capitulated a week earlier, that Tito's troops cut off a column of soldiers and collaborators: the "famous" battle of Poljana, won by the partisans, was the last battle of World War II in Europe. Massacres of soldiers and collaborators ensued, especially of the Prinz Eugen around Celje (Cilli) and Ranna, the Handschar and Skanderbeg, but also 1.GD whose officers, including Ludwig Kübler, were accused of war crimes and executed after the war.

The German forces engaged in the Balkans did not necessarily have the choice of whom to surrender to. Unlike this very young soldier, not all of them ended up in American or British PoW camps. A good number of *Gebirgsjäger* remained prisoners of the Yugoslav partisans for only a few days before they "disappeared." (DR, Colorization)

Having just landed in Britain, German PoWs line up. Among them, visible behind the Kriegsmarine coastal artilleryman in the foreground, is at least one man from the mountain troops, possibly GAR191, even if the color of the branch of arm on the shoulder strap does not appear to be red. (IWM)

The Campaign in the West, 1944–45

On the Western Front, mountain troops were engaged on the Franco-Italian and the Franco-German borders. Engaged in Normandy in 1944, GAR191 from 91.(Luftlande) ID (whose operational existence was brief) must be mentioned, as well as Brandenburg units in the southwest of France, who were not mountain specialized, but who took advantage of their time in the Pyrenees to develop their training in this type of terrain. Before the fighting on the Franco-Italian border, mountain units took part in counter-guerrilla operations in France, as soon as the first Maquis (Resistance) groups were established, particularly after the defection of Italy and the Allied invasion of September 1943.

Counter-guerilla Operations in France

Mention must be made of a mountain unit (as outlined in the previous chapter) which stayed in France in the Auvergne to perfect its training, on karstic terrain similar to that found in Bosnia, especially in the Cevennes: the Kroatische SS-Frw.-Geb.-Div., the future Handschar. Its advance parties arrived on July 1, 1943 in Puy-en-Velay (Haute-Loire, department 43) where they set up a transit camp (*Durchgangslager*) and the *Div.Stab*. This is where the name Handschar—the divisional journal was known as *Handzar*—was thought up and where volunteers swore their oath of loyalty to the Führer and to the Poglavnik Pavelic (the title used by the Croat leader, Ante Pavelić). By the end of the month 15,000 men had joined the unit. On August 9, the new divisional commander, Sauberzweig, took over his command at Mende. Fearful of sabotage—he didn't trust the local populace, viz. the supposed presence of *maquisards* (Resistance fighters) in the region backed by the Allies—he ordered his troops to take protective measures and to retaliate against Communists and Gaullists (but with execution only permitted on his orders).

Training began at the end of August, but recurring issues hampered progress: weakness of the officers (often under-strength) and *Volkdeutsche* who had served in the Austro-Hungarian army and were unfit for armed service. Consequently, 11 companies had no company commanders, five company commanders were subpar, and the artillery had no section leader. The 2,800 Catholic Croats moreover felt they were neglected compared with the Muslims from Bosnia, a region that was part of Croatia, or with the Albanian-speakers from the Kosovo. The opinion of the German officers of the *Mujo*, a nickname (and a common local first name) given to the Croat volunteers, vacillated between good and inadequate.

The officers discovered another potent criterion unknown in the Waffen-SS at the time: the imams. Identified by the Ulemas in Sarajevo, they were trained in Berlin-Babelsberg as "chaplains"—and therefore religious authorities—and assisted in turning the young recruits into effective SS soldiers. Their mentor was the Grand Mufti of Jerusalem, Amin Hadj el-Husseini (for two decades virulently anti-British, and incidentally Yasser Arafat's great-uncle), who visited them at le Puy-en-Velay and who saw many parallels between Islam and National Socialism.

At the end of August 1943, the engineer battalion (SS-Geb.-Pionier-Bataillon 13), with two companies, was transferred to Villefranche-de-Rouergue in the Aveyron department. On September 17, shortly after midnight, a mutiny broke out, led by a group of four conspirators, former Catholic or Communist partisans (who had infiltrated the division on Tito's instructions), attracting a large number of recruits. Five German officers were ruthlessly executed, including the battalion commander, *SS-Hauptsturmführer* Kuntz. By

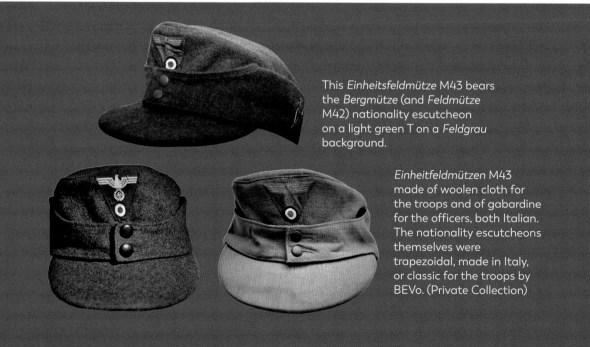

This *Einheitsfeldmütze* M43 bears the *Bergmütze* (and *Feldmütze* M42) nationality escutcheon on a light green T on a *Feldgrau* background.

Einheitfeldmützen M43 made of woolen cloth for the troops and of gabardine for the officers, both Italian. The nationality escutcheons themselves were trapezoidal, made in Italy, or classic for the troops by BEVo. (Private Collection)

An infantry officer on horseback approaching the southern bank of the Durance River, to the west of Embrun, identified by its cathedral and in the foreground its steel bridge.

This master sergeant poses with Grand Morgon in the background, its summit in clouds.

This is clearly Res.-GJR1 of 157.Res.-Div intervening in the Hautes Alpes after Italian troops in France had been disarmed in September 1943. The unit was followed by an amateur photographer. It was manifestly still made up of disparate elements: mainly mountain troops but also infantry, a normal situation for a depot battalion. These photographs were taken above the Durance, in the Embrun–Gap region, Chorges–Prunières, as well as the valley of la Blanche.

Two very young muleteers wearing M42 *Feldblusen* made in 1943. They are part of a mule train carrying ammunition.

An extremely rare photograph of the 157. during operations against the Maquis in the Glières and Vercors regions. This is a light column, *le. Kolonne*, transporting jerrycans and ammunition. The soldiers wear a combination of uniforms: *Feldmütze* 35, and *Bergmütze* without edelweiss, typical of the division at the time. (DR Reibert)

During the winter of 1943/4, anti-Maquis operations continued in the Dauphiné, Savoie, and Ain departments, regardless of weather or terrain. (Lenz Archives)

the end of the morning of the 17th, the mutiny had been put down, its leaders killed or imprisoned. Sauberzweig—who had envisaged the Resistance supporting the mutineers as they had expected, which was not the case—proclaimed martial law in Villefranche-de-Rouergue and all non-Germans were temporarily disarmed. Fourteen mutineers were shot before the assembled battalion.

On September 19, Himmler ordered the division to be repatriated to a more "Germanic" environment, Neuhammer camp—suspected Balkan Jews and North African Muslims had been spotted near the Handschar cantonments in Villefranche de Rouergue—northeast of Dresden in Silesia. A fifteenth mutineer was executed there and several hundred unreliable soldiers were rounded up and sent to concentration camps. Unlike other units, this training phase in France was not used advantageously in the struggle against the French Maquis.

In the Alps, in the spring of 1943, French Resistance fighters began assembling on the Glières plateau, an area where they could receive parachute drops. 157. Reserve-Division—a major unit comprising a series of depots and training units (*Ersatz und Ausbildung*) which had become Reserve and been incorporated into the Feldheer, the active army, on July 27, 1943—detached smaller units in support of French (Vichy) forces maintaining order. This type of operation continued until the end of the year. The dual vocation of training recruits and carrying out operations against the Maquis was sometimes difficult to manage.

In August 1943, in readiness for the Italian defection, the division assembled in Grenoble, in preparation of the disarmament of the Italian units, Operation *Achse* (initially *Alarich*). The radio announcement made by Marshal Badoglio on September 8 triggered the intervention of two battalions from Res.-GJR1 (99. and II./98.Res.GJB) in the Montgenèvre, Mont-Cenis, and Fréjus passes against the Alpini, who refused to lay down their arms. The Germans attacked from several directions,

During operations against the Vercors Maquis, elements of the Sicherheitdienst (SD) were attached to 157.Res.-Div., like this sergeant on the right. The SD was responsible for most of the massacres of *maquisards* and civilians.

112

Faced with massed uprisings by the French Resistance and intensifying operations by the Italian *partigiani* (partisans), the Polizei were called in. Here *Gebirgs-Polizisten* rest after an engagement. The man on the right is wearing a camouflaged Italian canvas anorak. (R. Eirermann Archives)

from France and from Italy, but were unable to prevent the sabotage of the Mont-Cenis tunnel. However, reconstruction was soon under way using Italian prisoners.

Several other subunits were used for disarmament operations in France, in the Embrun region. The division thus covered several French departments including the Savoie and Dauphiné. It also had to act in the Ain department. In early 1944, Major General Karl Pflaum's task was collecting information, using patrols along the roads, in the villages, in the mountains, on skis if necessary, making use of police reports and any denunciations. Operation *Korporal* in the Ain department, from February 5–13, 1944, enabled him to prepare his personnel for the anti-partisan struggle. By the end of January 1944, bands of *maquisards* on the Plateau des Glières were equipping themselves with skis taken from ski resorts.

The approaching Allied landings in the west caused tension on both sides. 157. Reserve-Division was subordinated to LXIV.AK. Once its deployment with the Milice and the GMR police (Groupes Mobiles de Réserve, forerunner to the modern Compagnies républicaines de sécurité, or CRS, the police intervention units), who were understrength to fight the Maquis, 157.Res.-Div. planned and carried out Operation *Hoch-Savoyen* (*Upper Savoy*) from March 26–31, 1944. The artillery began ranging in on March 25. The *Kampfgruppe* was organized around Res.GJR15, and comprised some 4,000 men, including French police, against 450 Resistance fighters who had adopted the pennant and the traditions of the 27e

Operation *Himmelsfahrt* saw 5.GD/GJR100 Sturmkompanie engaged in the Mont Blanc massif. Captain Siegle, killed during the operation, poses with a heavy machine-gun group from his assault company. (Novak Archives)

A group from Sturmkompanie 5.GD (GJR 100) is mounted on this Italian Semovente assault gun of the Geb.-PzJg-Abt.85. (Novak Archives)

Colonel Ludwig Stautner commanded Kampfgruppe Aosta. He was awarded the Knight's Cross in Norway in the spring of 1940. He was also a *Bergführer*. (DR, Colorization)

Bataillon de Chasseurs Alpins. The division's mission was to take the plateau, annihilate the *maquisards* and prevent any further activity in the region.

The *Kampfgruppe* attacked with four *Gebirgsjäger* battalions on March 26, but without sufficient liaison between Stab 157 and the Vichyist forces. About 130 *maquisards* were able to escape from the plateau; however, a number of them were captured and executed in the ensuing days, including almost all the leaders. But overall, the division considered the operation a failure, and "Les Glières" became a symbol of French patriotism. The division then began preparing for Operation *Frühling* (*Spring*) from April 7–17, 1944, in the Ain department around Saint-Claude.

The Normandy landings caused a revival of patriotism in France and thus an overall increase in operations and massed uprisings, which overextended the anti-Maquis forces. Inspired by the dynamism of Les Glières, another group was gaining prominence, between the Isère and Drôme departments, on the Plateau of the Vercors, where some 4,500 assembled *maquisards* reconstituted the Chasseurs Alpins and Cuirassier units.

Operation *Bettina* took place from July 14–23, primarily forcing the Resistance to disperse. Airborne, police and SD elements were engaged alongside 157.Res.-Div, the SD being incorporated into the *Gebirgsjäger* and, it seems, responsible for most of the massacres perpetrated against French combatants and civilians alike.

After leaving the Italian front, these two *Gebirgsjäger* of 5.GD along the French-Italian border are wearing the reversible two-piece overall, *Windbluse* and *Windhose*. (Franz Moll Archives)

This *Oberjäger* (Sergeant), sharing cigarettes with some Alpini, is wearing the KRETA cuff band.

157.Res.-Div also took part in the anti-partisan struggle in northern Italy. From July 17, elements in training near Bardonnechia in Italy—four companies from Res.-GJR1 (I./Res.-GJB98)—were kept in reserve for almost four weeks during the Italo-German operation, Operation *Nachtigall* (*Nightingale*), against Italian partisans from the Val Chisone brigade. Res. GJB99 was involved in the same operation deploying southeastward from the Montgenèvre Pass.

A word now on how the Germans interpreted the Maquis and the French populace. The 19. Armee *Kriegestagebuch* (war diary) dated August 7 explained that the term "terrorist" should henceforth be forbidden, because they were now facing structured units, with uniformed officers acting in the rear of army groups. Moreover, the possibility of a "popular uprising" by people with a passionate temperament, far removed from an apathetic French population, had to be taken into account as a similar remark was made about the *Banden* on August 20).

The Allied landing in Provence on August 15 abruptly changed the situation across southeastern France. On the 18th, Army Group G ordered all forces in the southwest of France to deploy northeast before they were cut off by the linkup between Allied forces from Normandy and from Provence.

At the same time, 157.Res.-Div was ordered to fall back toward the Franco-Italian border, whilst at the same time ensuring it protected elements of 19. Armee withdrawing in the eastern Rhône Valley. However, events soon overtook these orders.

Indeed, on August 19, the Haute-Savoie and Savoie Maquis completed the liberation of their departments. At the beginning of the month, 157.Res.-Div had set off against the Maquis in the Oisans, after the Vercors uprising had been crushed. Assessing that American vanguards were en route, it was forced to withdraw toward Grenoble then Pont-de-Claix, burning villages on the way. Using the Route Napoléon, opened up by the Maquis, the Americans entered Gap on August 20—they had crossed the Durance at Sisteron-Digne the day before, nearly two months ahead of schedule—without a shot being fired, and Grenoble on the 22nd. The Maquis pursued 157. Res.-Div. into the Maurienne and Tarentaise valleys, driving it toward the Franco-Italian border but unable to prevent a hundred hostages being massacred.

In September, 157.Res.-Div was engaged on the Franco-Italian border, using former French fortifications as strongpoints. It took part in halting French and American units in the Briançonnais and stabilized the front before being relieved by 5.GD. It then moved into Italy to evolve into 8.GD (see earlier chapter "Italy, 1943–45").

The Second Battle of the Alps, 1944–45

With the Allies landing in Provence on August 15, 1944 the Germans decided the next day, on the one hand, to withdraw most of their forces (Army Group G) back north up the Rhône Valley, and on the other, to have the remaining units pivot and deploy in defensive positions facing west along the Franco-Italian border (*Alpen-Stellung*, Alpine Line). Including defending the rear against Italian Resistance operations, this was entrusted to LXXV.AK (Lieutenant General Hans Schlemmer).

157. Reserve-Division, engaged up until then against the French Maquis (Vercors and Glières) and the Italian partisans (the big spring and summer operations of 1944), started pulling its units back on August 19 in order to occupy the northern part of the line.

To ensure the elements engaged near Grenoble could withdraw to the frontier, 90.PzGren-Div., reinforced by Hochgebirgs-Bataillon 4 (Hoch 4, Captain Andreas Schönleben), was deployed as a recovery unit, to control the passes before detaching a *Kampfgruppe* toward Grenoble. Hoch 4 then joined 148.ID in the southern sector between Ventimiglia and Alassio, with its command post at Dolceacqua. The high-mountain *Jäger* pursued Italian partisans and took part in defending the coast. After the Provence landings, the battalion was sent back into France, just across the border, to eliminate the Maquis formed in the Nice and Menton hinterland (the Vésubie and Tinée regions).

On August 20, the reconnaissance platoon that had entered France through Menton clashed with partisans at the Banquettes Pass. In September, the battalion harassed the US 509th Parachute Infantry Battalion set up at Saint-Martin Vésubie, sustaining losses in the process. With the first snows in early October, advancing in the mountains, already difficult in the rugged terrain, now became almost impossible. Several *Jäger* were killed in an avalanche on the 31st. From November 1944 onward, only the border crest was held, by the Italian Littorio Division.

At the end of August 1944, 5.GD (Lieutenant General August Max-Günther Schrank), retained until then in the Führer-Reserve (literally "reserve of officers", waiting for an assignment, a general term applied to units and individuals) of Army Group South, had recouped its strength after the campaign on the Gustav and Gothic Lines. It occupied the passes and relieved the Italian Littorio in the north between the Petit Saint-Bernard and Mount Viso, and enabled 90.PGD to break off on September 4. Some of its elements (see earlier chapter "Italy, 1943–45") remained in the Rimini sector until the end of November before reaching the Alps. On September 13, overall coordination of the anti-partisan struggle east of the border became the responsibility of Army Group Ligurien.

These *Gebirgsjäger* have arrived in Alsace, in the foothills of the Vosges, and have found shelter in a lean-to shed. (DR)

At the beginning of November, 157. Reserve-Division became a *Gebirgs-Division* and was relieved by 5.GD and the Italian 2nd Infantry Division Littorio two weeks later.

The bulk of 157. Reserve-Division's officers, around 90 percent, had been transferred for disciplinary reasons after the atrocities committed in France by SD elements. It reached the Apennines as 8.GD at the end of November 1944. Lieutenant General Paul Schricker had replaced Lieutenant General Karl Pflaum in late August.

Diverted from the Ligurian coast after being decimated in Russia, 34.ID under Major General Theo-Helmut Lieb, relieved 148 Res.-Div on September 15, 1944. Because of its task, this division was partly equipped for the mountains. Apart from the combat units mentioned above, other "mountain" units were engaged in this sector, either on the border, or in the rear:

- Hochgebirgsbataillon 3, incorporated initially in the 157.Res.-Div order of battle, became a divisional organic battalion at the end of December 1944; this battalion was engaged in particular on the Larche Pass;

- Gebirgsjäger-Lehrbataillon Mittenwald, composed mainly of instructors and high-mountain specialists, was set up at the beginning of June 1944 for future operations on the Abruzzi (Gothic Line); it was attached temporarily to Kampfgruppe Meeralpen;

- Kampfgruppe Aosta under Colonel Stautner: this temporary Germano-Italian tactical group, allocated to defending the Petit Saint-Bernard and passes on either side of Mont Blanc, was made up of I./3° Alpini Regiment, II./GJR100, Div.-Sturmkp from 5.GD, and part of Geb.-PzJg-Abt.85;

- Germano-Italian Kampfgruppe Maddalena (Major then Lieutenant Colonel Freiherr Franz von Ruffin, former commander of Hoch 4), organized around Hoch 4;

- Gebirgsjäger-Regiment Meeralpen shared a regimental command post with Hoch 4. Created on October 24, 1944, it was part of Army Group Ligurien. It

These two prisoners from "Nord" are teenagers. Their uniforms are faded and their winter equipment is inadequate.

117

Like all light infantry divisions, "Nord" received a Sturmgeschütze III allocation. The half-track in the photo presupposes that an American column has been intercepted between the Vosges and Hunsrück. (DR)

joined forces with Geb.-Lehrbataillon Mittenwald and was detached from December 26–29 to 148.Res.-Div. (LI.Geb.-AK) by AOK14 which was directing a counterattack in the Serchio Valley, in the Apennines;

- Polizei-Regiment Bozen frequently displayed the edelweiss because of its personnel's origins: the Alto Adige/Südtirol. This regiment was operational in the anti-partisan struggle in the Italian mountains.

After several reorganizations due to the staggered arrival of units from 5.GD and 34.ID, the gaps were occupied by Italian elements, principally the Monterosa (mountain) and Littorio (infantry/mountain mix) divisions formed in Germany and partly equipped with German matériel.

The secondary front, Westalpen, intended to prevent the Allies from breaking through behind 10. and 14. Armeen, was stabilized until the end of the war: weather and geography were in control: "In winter, the Alps defend themselves," said Field Marshal Kesselring.

Patrols, ambushes, occasionally holding fortified positions, and conducting high-risk resupply missions (with the danger of avalanches) on the former Alpine Maginot Line or its Italian counterpart, stationed at between 2,000 and 3,000 meters—made up the *Gebirgstruppen*'s daily life on the *Alpen-Stellung*. Both *GJR*s were in the line, 100. to the north and 85. to the south. Capturing the high points, just as indispensable for defense as they were for resuming the offensive on the French side, entailed ruthless hand-to-hand fighting on Mont Froid (2,819 meters) between February 6–8.

Note also "the highest fighting of the war" (3,400 meters) occurred on February 17, 1945 in the Mont Blanc range when Sturmkompanie 5.GD carried out Operation *Himmelfahrt* (*Ascension* [of Christ]). At -13°F, in the morning mist, it tried in vain to capture French positions in the Col du Midi and the Refuge du Requin.

The Germans broke off in good order on April 24, 1945 in order to reach the *Alpenfestung*, the Alpine Redoubt. They applied drastic methods to protect themselves from partisan attacks and laid down their arms at Fiferoni, in the Turin region which the Allies had reached before them.

Operation *Nordwind*, Alsace 1945

Operation *Nordwind* (*North Wind*) was first envisaged as an alternative to Operation *Wacht am Rhein* (*Rhine Watch*), the counteroffensive in the Ardennes (the Battle of the Bulge); then as a fall operation to try and retain the initiative in the West by preventing the Allies from drawing troops from Alsace-Lorraine to send them to Bastogne; then to make the most of the major waterway that is the Rhine. Operation *Nordwind* was launched on December 31, 1944, when *Wacht am Rhein* had already been stopped.

The definitive plan of attack had been decided on Christmas Day by the Führer himself. During the night of January 4/5, 1945, 553.ID infiltrated covertly to form a bridgehead on the Rhine, to the north of Gambsheim, level with Haguenau. The aim of this was to introduce powerful elements to the north of Strasbourg, to support the attack and the fighting taking place around Haguenau, as well as maintaining a corridor to cross back through if necessary

Particularly between Haguenau and Wissembourg, from January 8–20, 1945, Operation *Nordwind* was the last German large-scale operation on the Western Front. Two mountain divisions were engaged, both coming from the Northern Front (see earlier chapter "Norway and Finland, 1942–45"). This action continued between the Moselle and the Saar, where the Germans tried to contain the American thrust toward the Rhine along the Moselle Valley. The group was commanded by the new Army Group Oberrhein (high command of the Upper Rhine) under Himmler's direct command. During the fall the terrain had been inundated; the waterlogged ground then froze and temperatures plummeted below freezing.

In coordination with *Nordwind*, operations in the south of Alsace prolonged the Allied offensive. 19. Armee, retreating from the South of France, had positioned itself defensively in Alsace and was then bottled up at the end of 1944 inside the Colmar Pocket (*Brückenkopf Elsaß*, the Alsace bridgehead as it was referred to by the Germans). The Allies had reached the Rhine at Mulhouse on November 19 and on the 23rd at Strasbourg (General Leclerc de Hautecloque and his 2e Division Blindée). Leclerc did not immediately cross the Rhine but attempted to reduce the pocket and advance north to completely liberate Alsace.

2.GD had left Norway at the end of December 1944, after traveling by train down to the Oslo region. It reached Arhus in Denmark by sea and then Hamburg, before transferring directly to Neuf-Brisach on the banks of the Rhine, then Gueberschwihr, to join the defenders of the Colmar Pocket. Shortly after it arrived, the division was engaged around Mulhouse on January 24, 1945, facing the French 1er Corps, which took part in the Franco-American Operation *Cheerful* launched on the 20th.

Although the Allies were unable to annihilate the Colmar Pocket, they did succeed in drawing the German reserves south, because the Germans feared an attack on Strasbourg, like Operation *Tauziehen* (*Tug of War*), which had taken the Allies to Erstein, 10 kilometers southwest of the symbolic city.

On January 22, the French 2e Corps and elements of the US Seventh Army—254th Infantry Regiment of the 3rd Infantry Division—attacked the salient at Erstein. From January 24 to February 2, GJR136 from 2.GD was in contact at Jebsheim where there was heavy street fighting with the French 5e DB and the 1er Régiment de Chasseurs Parachutistes. The

This *Einheitsfeldmütze* M43 of a Waffen-SS officer is a later model made of Italian gabardine cloth, with a woven BEVo troop escutcheon with white piping on the front. (Private collection)

village changed hands three times in nine days, but after February 2, the battle shifted to the plain nearby, particularly because 654. Schwere Panzerjäger-Abteilung had arrived with Jagdpanther tank destroyers.

Eventually, the remnants of 2.GD and a hodge-podge of residual elements managed to cross the Rhine at Neuf-Brisach and to move north. Initially in 1. Armee's reserve, the division redeployed into defensive positions by going through the Saar and relieving 559. Volksgrenadier-Division at Bitche. It successfully drove off several attacks before reaching the region to the south of Trèves (Trier).

6. Gebirgs-Division der Waffen-SS Nord under Major General Karl-Heinrich Brenner, which had also arrived from Norway at the end of 1944, was in turn engaged in January/February 1945 in the Northern Vosges, attached to Sturmgruppe 2 attacking to the west of the Vosges (Sturmgruppe 1 was to the east). It had transited via Denmark to be issued new equipment (it was at last issued MG 42s, for example). It had suffered heavy losses and, to compensate, had received some very young recruits, some of them *Volksdeutsche*.

With its arrival in the Saarland, it was the freshest unit in the Wehrmacht in the West. It emerged from the Northern Vosges to the east of Bitche, within XC.AK, in order to secure the main crest line of the Vosges and to open the breach at Saverne, the strategic corridor between Alsace and the Moselle, bypassing 257. and 361.VGDen which had attacked on January 1 and had advanced 15 or so kilometers to Wingen-sur-Moder and Wimmenau.

Kampfgruppe Schreiber (I./ and III./SS-GJR12 Michael Gaißmair) in a surprise attack and with no artillery preparation, took Wingen-sur-Moder on January 4, without difficulty, facing the US 179th and 45th Thunderbird Infantry Divisions. On the 5th, the US 70th infantry Division, engaged up until then on the Rhine plain, counterattacked but failed to dislodge Nord's *Jäger* who gradually began running out of ammunition, cut off as they were from their supply lines.

When these were re-established, the *Kampfgruppe* remnants of 205 men fell back on friendly lines. On January 14, 1945, the US 45th ID resumed its attack

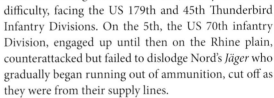

The final development of combat dress, the so-called *Leibermuster* model, is shown here. It is still unclear which units were issued with this. At least one *Jäger-Division*, 114.JgD, seems to have received it; the division fought in the Balkans alongside 1.GD, but distribution could have transpired elsewhere. This camouflage pattern was to replace all Wehrmacht and Waffen-SS issues with complete fleece-lined winter and summer collections. The jacket tucked into the trousers enables the waist details to be seen. (Private collection, reenactment with contemporary equipment)

farther east, level with Wingen-sur-Moder, and tried in vain to take the heights at the village of Reipertswiller, held by SS-GJR11 Reinhard Heydrich.[1]

The regiment carried out the Finnish tactic of the *Motti* (see earlier chapter "Norway and Finland, 1942–45") which enabled it to surround some American companies which could not be extricated by their own forces and thus 50 GIs went off into captivity.

But the "Nord" had suffered heavy losses, notably because of the air attacks and had to fall back on its starting point to be allocated a new mission during the night of January 6/7. The Allied VI Corps shadowed this rearward movement but settled defensively on the Bitche–Bischwiller–Moder–Haguenau line—envisaged ever since the beginning of the month[2]—in order to reorganize, two divisions having been freed up by the success at Bastogne. Allied units engaged in Upper Alsace fell back during the night of January 20/21, 1945, untroubled thanks to execrable weather. The Germans took advantage of this and followed in order to retake ground along the Rhine and reestablish links with the Gambsheim bridgehead mentioned above. The original idea of forcing the breach at Saverne proved a necessity for the German command and all units resumed their advance in the direction of Bischwiller to the east of the sector. At the same time, "Nord" attacked during the night of the 24th/25th in the direction of Bischholtz and Schillersdorf. After initial success, the division had to halt its advance. On the same day, January 25, 1945, Hitler ordered a halt to *Nordwind*. On the 27th, he deployed three divisions to the Eastern Front.

"Nord" remained in position in the Northern Vosges for a month, to the southeast of Bitche. Between February 28 and March 2, it joined LXXXII.AK in the Hermeskeil–Reichsfeld sector, in the Hunsrück range. It was reunited there with 2.GD, positioning itself to the east of the Ruwer. The terrain was very hilly, snowbound and temperatures were subzero, weather conditions worthy of Karelia.

The US 94th ID had set up a bridgehead on the Saar. The Germans, unable to regain the initiative, attempted to cut the American supply lines, From March 5–8, guarded on the flanks by the remnants of 2.GD (II./GJR137 under Captain von Strachwitz)—in the process of attempting to retake the "Auf der Kupp" crest, near Niederzerf—and of the 256. Volksgrenadier-Division, "Nord" tried unsuccessfully to recapture villages and key points to the east of the Ruwer.

After suffering heavy losses, despite supporting fire from SS-GAR6 and the Sturmgeschützen, "Nord" fell back north of Hermeskeil, along the Hunsrück range. It had lost almost all its matériel, destroyed or out of gas. SS-GJR12 left the division for a mission on the east bank of the Rhine, near Mannheim. The *Stab* with the remnants of the division (about the size of a *Kampfgruppe* around SS-GJR11) continued falling back to the north-northeast. It held its positions level with Boppard-Brodenbach between the Moselle and the Rhine, on the right-hand bank of the Rhine to the west of Wiesbaden and to the east of Koblenz. Finally, now in 7. Armee's reserve, "Nord" withdrew in April toward Büdingen north of Frankfurt (Hesse) where some 800 *Jäger* were captured by the Americans.

2.GD, still under command of LXXXII.AK, retreated to Bavaria and the Tyrol. The division finished the war in captivity in the Salzburg region.

1 Attributed to the regiment on June 4, 1942, on Hitler's order, GJR11 having been formed in Prague with No. 6.
2 Including abandoning Strasbourg which, in the worst-case scenario, would have been retaken by the Germans. De Gaulle opposed this and the French defended the symbol of the reconquest which began in Chad (with the Leclerc's so-called Oath of Kufra), with, notably, the Alsace-Lorraine brigade under Colonel André Malraux together with the 159e Régiment d'Infanterie Alpine from the Alps.

| Afterword

Recent studies of the reasons for their "superhuman" qualities have proved that mountain troops used methamphetamines, sometimes often, in order to develop confidence in themselves, and overcome tiredness over long periods and long distances, especially during times of extreme cold and great privation. Pervitine appears to have been one of the most commonly used drugs, issued in tablet or chocolate form (known as *Panzerschokolade*). Did this perhaps coin the term *Glückshormone*, the "happiness hormone," a term for chocolate used today in the Bundeswehr?

The longer-term effects were soon detected—addiction and psychotic behavior—and its use was gradually restricted. Some soldiers remained addicted after the war. These remarks are not intended to minimize the true operational abilities of the *Gebirgstruppen* who were recognized by their adversaries as "elite troops," but to consider the use of drugs as a tool for the regime's propaganda.

These 13 chapters, across two volumes, bookended by timelines, appendices and indexes, will enable readers to familiarize themselves with units often mentioned and encountered in numerous books. The need to condense the texts has of course, in some instances, led to a cul-de-sac. Each of the units described indeed follows a unique path, in very different theaters, very often far from the mountains where they should have been deployed.

A Finnish reenactment group has adopted the theme of the "Nord" division, underlining the variety of dress, realistically shown here: padded camouflaged/white ensemble, but more frequently, it would seem, the *Mantel* was still much used. (DR, gaissmair.net)

A classic view of the last of the *Gebirgsjäger* fighters, in May 1945, shortly before capture, coming out of their foxholes: the *Windjacke*, the weapon, the *Zeltbahn*, are all covered with mud. (DR)

In Scandinavia captured German troops remained in their subunits, under command of their officers. The nationality insignia, and sometimes the decorations, were denazified.

The term "extreme conditions," mentioned more than a few times in these pages, was often applied to their environment. But words on a page belie the frozen hell of the Eastern Front in the depths of winter, for example. The living and combat conditions which the author has attempted to capture, reveal the near-superhuman character of the *Gebirgstruppen*. Indeed, few combatants were able to bear so stoically such extreme conditions during World War II.

The planners never stopped. The Germans are recognized as having been at the forefront of technological advances in 1944/5. This Focke-Achgelis Fa 223 "Drachen" two-rotor helicopter—here captured by the Americans—took part in trials transporting Geb.-Gesch.36 howitzers up into the mountains, slung beneath the fuselage. (DR)

| Sources

Aichner, Ernst (Hrsg.), *Deutsche Gebirgstruppen, vom 1. Weltkrieg bis zur Gegenwart*, Sonderaustellung des bayerischen Armeemuseums Ingolstadt, 1983.

Béraud, Henri & Yves Béraud, *La deuxième Bataille des Alpes 1944/1945*, Hors-série de la Gazette des Uniformes n° 20, Régi'Arm, Paris, 2005.

Béraud, Henri, *Bataille des Alpes*, Album Mémorial Juin 1940–1944/45, Editions Heimdal, Bayeux, 1987.

Béraud, Henri, *La Seconde Guerre mondiale dans les Hautes-Alpes et l'Ubaye*, Société d'Etudes des Hautes-Alpes, 1990.

Bernage, Georges & François de Lannoy, *Dictionnaire historique: Les divisions de l'Armée de Terre allemande*, Editions Heimdal, 1997.

Bernage, Georges & François de Lannoy, *Dictionnaire historique: La Luftwaffe et la Waffen-SS, 1939–1945*, Editions Heimdal, 1998.

Body, Derek & Wayne Turner, *Gebirgsjäger in the West, Official Briefing: 2.Gebirgsdivision and 6.SS-Gebirgsdivision "Nord" on the Western Front, 1945*, Flames of War, 2014.

Bruns, Friedrich, *Westeuropa 1944–45, Band 1, Die "Mittelmeer" Invasion (Einsatz der Panzer-Brtigade 106 FHH)*, Celle, Selbstverlag, 1984.

Corbatti, Sergio & Marco Nava *Karstjäger! Guerriglia e controguerriglia nell'OZAK 1943–45*, Associazione MADM, Brianza Viva, Saregno, 2005.

De Loverdo, Costa *Les Maquis Rouges des Balkans*, Stock, 1967.

Die deutschen Gebirgsdivisionen im zweiten Weltkrieg, Allgemeine schweizerische Militärzeitschrift (ASMZ), 1948.

Greiner, Helmut & Percy Ernst Schramm, *Kriegstagebuch des Oberkommandos der Wehrmacht 1939–1945*, Bernard und Graefe Verlag, München, 1982.

Gunter, Georg, *Die deutschen Skijäger: von den Anfängen bis 1945*, Podzun-Pallas-Verlag, 1993.

Haupt, Werner, *Leningrad Wochow Kurland: Bildbericht der Heeresgruppe Nord 1941–1945*, Podzun-Pallas-Verlag, Friedberg, 1976.

Hinze, Rolf, *Das Ostfrontdrama 1944: Rückzugskämpfeder Heeresgruppe Mitte*, Motorbuch Verlag, Stuttgart, 1997.

Kaltenegger Roland, *Ludwig Kübler: General der Gebirgstruppe*, Motorbuch Verlag, Stuttgart, 1998.

Kaltenegger, Roland, *Kampf der Gebirgsjäger um die Westalpen und den Semmering: Chronik der 8. und 9. Gebirgs-Division ("Kampfgruppe Semmering")*, Leopold Stocker Verlag, Graz-Stuttgart, 1987.

Kern, Erich *Generalfeldmarschall Schörner*, Verlag, K.W. Schütz KG, Preußich Oldendorf, 1976.

Knabe, Konrad, *Die schweigende Front: Dietl's Kampf im hohen Norden 1940–1944*, Druffel-Verlag, Leoni am Starnberger See, 1979.

Kosar, Franz, *Gebirgsartillerie: Geschichte, Waffen, Organisation*, Motorbuch Verlag, Stuttgart, 1987.

Kost, Werner *Gebirgsjäger in Libyens Wüste*, Bruno Langer Verlag Esslingen, 1988.

Kumm, Otto, *Vorwärts Prinz Eugen, Geschichte der 7. SS-Freiwilligen-Division "Prinz Eugen,"* Munin-Verlag GmbH, Osnabrück, 1978.

Lanz, Hubert, *Gebirgsjäger: Die 1. Gebirgsdivision 1935–1945*, Verlag Hans-Henning Podzun, Bad Nauheim, 1954.

Lazzero, Ricciotti, *Le SS italiane. Storia dei 20000 che giurarono fedeltà a Hitler*, Rizzoli Editore, Milano, 1982.

Lepre, George, *Himmler's Bosnian Division: The Waffen-SS Handschar Division, 1943–1945*, Schiffer Military History, Atglen PA, 1997.

Offizier im grossdeutschen Heer, Merkworte für die Berufswahl, Kriegsausgabe, 1942.

Ott, Ernst-Ludwig, *Die Spielhahnjäger 1940–1945, Bilddokumentation der 97. Jäger-Division*, Podzun-Pallas-Verlag, 1982.

Ott, Ernst-Ludwig, *Jäger am Feind: Geschichte und Opfergang der 97. Jäger-Division*, Selbstverlag der Kameradschaft der Spielhahnjäger e.V., München, 1966.

Perny, Pierre, C. Siedel, J. Voltzenlogel, A.Debs, C.Walther & L. M. Pommois, *Opération Nordwind: Alsace du Nord janvier 1945*, Historica Spécial Alsace, Editions Heimdal, 1992.

Ringel, Julius, *Hurra, die Gams!: Ein Gedenkbuch für die Soldaten der 5. Gebirgsdivision*, Leopold Stocker Verlag, Graz et Göttingen, 1975.

Schmitz, Peter & Klaus-Jürgen Thies, *Die Truppenkennzeichen der Verbände und Einheiten der deutschen Wehrmacht und Waffen-SS im Zweiten Weltkrieg 1939–1945*, Biblio Verlag, Osnabrück, 2000.

Schröder, Karl, *Dort wo der Adler haust: Geschichte des Hochgebirgsjäger-Bataillons 4. Eine Chronik aus den Jahren, 1943–1945*, (Eigenverlag) Owschlag, 1989.

Scipion, Jacques & Yves Bastien, *AFRIKAKORPS, les tenues tropicales de l'armée allemande, 1938–1945*, Histoire & Collections, 1994.

Später, Helmut, *Die Brandenburger: Eine deutsche Kommandotruppe zbV 800*, Verlagsagentur Walther Angerer, München 86, 1978.

Steurich, Alfred, *Gebirgsjäger im Bild: 6. SS Gebirgsdivision Nord 1940–1945*, Munin-Verlag GmbH, Osnabrück, 1976.

Tessin, Georg, *Verbände und Truppen der deutschen Wehrmacht und Waffen-SS im Zweiten Weltkrieg 1939–1945*, Osnabrück, 1977–80.

Thomas, Nigel, Carlos Caballero Jurado & Simon McCouaig, *Wehrmacht Auxiliary Forces*, Men-At-Arms Series, Osprey Military, 1992.

Thomas, Nigel, Krunoslav Mikulan & Darko Pavlović, *Axis Forces in Yugoslavia 1941–45*, Men-at-Arms Series, Osprey, 1995.

Turinetti Di Priero, Alberto, *Nachtigall, L'operazione "Usignolo" nelle Valli Chisone, Susa, Germanascae Pellice, 29 luglio–12 agosto 1944*, Roberto Chiaramonte Editore, 1998.

Von Clausewitz, Carl, *Vom Kriege*.

Weinberger, Andreas, *Das gelbe Edelweiss*, Zentralverlag der NSDAP, Franz Eher Nachfolger, GmbH, München, 1943.

Wyler, Christian, *La longue marche de la Division 157 contre les maquis et les partisans 1942–1945*, Grancher, Paris, 2004.

Periodicals

39–45 Magazine various issues

Der Landser various issues

Die Gebirgstruppe, Federation of the German Mountain Troops' Association, various issues including a 1957 special edition

Die Wehrmacht various issues

Historica various issues

La Domenica del Corriere various issues

La Gazette des Uniformes various issues

Militaria Magazine various issues

Nordruf various issues

Signal various issues

Soldat und Waffe–Der II. Weltkrieg, Jahr-Verlag KG, 2000 Hamburg 1

Tempo various issues

Waffen-Revue various issues

Index

Albanian nationalists *also* Balli Kombetar resistance, 96, 102
Alpine Front, 66–7, 116, 118
Alps Mountains, 64, 68–69, 75, 87, 112, 116, 118, 121fn
Anzio landing, 62, 64

Belgrade, 79, 84, 88, 91–2, 94, 100, 104–105
Berlin, 33, 86, 94, 110
Bir Hakeim, 11–12
Bor-Komorowski, Gen, 36
Böttcher, Gen Karl, 105
Brack, Dr Victor, 77
Brazilian Expeditionary Force, 68
Brenner Pass, 15, 69
Brenner, Gen Karl-Heinrich, 120
Brest-Litovsk, 35
British Army, 6, 8–13, 15, 62, 67–68, 75, 95, 99
    Eighth Army, 6, 9; V Corps, 67; X Corps, 67; 6th AD, 75; Long Range Desert Group, 10
Budapest, 41, 90, 107
Bug River, 29–30, 36
Bulgarian forces, 79–80, 84, 86, 92, 103, 107
    1st Army, 79–80; 2nd Army, 92
Bulge, Battle of the, 119

Cap Bon, 16
Carpathian Mountains, 31, 37, 40, 87
Caucasus Mountains, 6, 8, 17–24, 26–28, 70–72, 102
Colmar Pocket, 119
Cossacks, 20, 33, 105fn
Crete, 9, 47, 61, 70
Crimea, 24, 28–31, 72
Czech forces, 37, 39, 57
    I Army Corps, 37; Resistance, 57

Danube River, 763, 88, 100, 104, 107
D-Day *see* Normandy landings
Demyansk Pocket, 28
Dietl, Gen Eduard, 47, 57–58

Dnieper River, 28–30
Dniester River, 29, 31
Don River, 17, 21, 27
Donets Basin *also* River, 17, 27, 29

Eglseer, Gen Karl, 47
El Alamein, first battle of, 12; second battle of, 13, 95

Felmy, Gen Hellmuth, 8, 107
Feuerstein, Gen Valentin, 68
Finnish Army, 32, 45–47, 50, 52, 55, 58–59, 121–122
French forces (Free French) 8–9, 12–15, 59, 62, 65, 69, 112–113, 115, 119
    1er Corps, 119; 2e Corps, 119
    2e DB, 119; 5e DB, 119
    Corps Expéditionnaire Français (CEF), 62, 65
    2e DI Marocaine, 62; 3e DI Algérienne, 62
    French Foreign Legion, 9, 14–15
    Maquis, 69, 112–116
French forces (Vichy), 8, 112–113
    GMR, 113; Milice, 113

Glières plateau, 112–114, 116
Globocnik, Odilo, 74
Gothic Line, 24, 28, 64–65, 67–69, 116–117
Grand Mufti of Jerusalem (Amin Hadj el-Husseini), 85, 103fn, 110
Greek forces, 95, 100
    Resistance, 95; EDES, 65; ELAS, 95
Gustav Line, 60, 62–63, 116

Halfaya Pass, 10, 13
Herr, Gen Traugott, 67–68
Himmler, Heinrich, 42, 71fn, 74, 80, 88–89, 94, 112
Hintersatz, Wilhelm (Harun-al-Raschid-Bey), 72–73
Hitler, Adolf, 8, 22, 29–30, 47, 67, 89, 92, 95, 97, 107, 121

Hungarian forces (1st Army), 35, 37

Islam *also* imams, 18fn, 72–73, 90–91, 93, 103fn, 110
Italian forces, 8, 11, 17, 27, 60, 64–65, 68–69, 71, 78, 81–82, 84–87, 95, 97–99, 111–113, 115–118
    8th Armata, 27; 9th Armata, 95; Italian Liberation Corps (ILC), 64; IV Corps, 84; XVII GaF, 71; 1st ID, 68; 2nd ID Littorio, 116–118; 4th MD Monterosa, 65, 118; 33rd ID Acqui, 99; 101st Mot.D Trieste Black Shirts, 11; 132nd AD Ariete D, 11; Resistance (partisans), 64–65, 69, 71, 85, 113, 115–116

Jodl, FM Alfred, 58
Jodl, Gen Ferdinand, 50

Karelia Front, 42, 44, 50, 55, 58, 70, 99, 121
Kasserine Pass, 13
Kerch Straits, 28
Keserović, Cmdt Dragutin, 80
Kirkenes, 47, 55, 57
Koch-Erpach, Gen, 39
Koenig, Gen Marie-Pierre, 12
Konev, Mar Ivan, 37
Konrad, Gen Rudolf, 17, 106
Kreysing, Gen Hans, 26–27
Kuban Front, 22, 79, 81; Peninsula, 24–25, 28, 30; River, 18, 23–25, 28–29, 96
Kübler, Josef Gen, 104–105, 107
Kübler, Ludwig Gen, 33, 70, 108
Kursk, battle of, 29, 32

Lake Lagoda, battles of, 26–28, 31
Lanz, Gen Karl Hubert, 23, 96–99, 106
Leningrad *also* Front, 25–27, 31, 47, 60, 65
Lieb, Gen Theo-Helmut, 117
Lindemann, Gen Georg, 27, 35

List, FM Wilhelm, 17, 79
Liza River, 44, 46, 55
Lüters, Gen Rudolf, 79

Maginot Line (Alpine), 118
Mannerheim Line, 50; President, 50
Mariopol, 28
Mersa Matruh, 12–13
Mga, 26–27, 31
Mieth, Gen Friedrich, 27, 29
Mihailović, Col Dragoljub "Draža," 78, 80
Mius River, 27, 29
Mont Blanc massif, 113, 117, 118
Monte Cassino, battles of, 60–65, 69
Monte Castellone, 62–63
Monte Sole, 69
Montgomery, Gen Bernard, 13
Mount Elbrus, 17–19, 21–22
Mount Ssmaschcho, 23
Muhasilovic, Abdullah, 93
Murmansk, 45, 50, 55

Nedic, Gen Milan, 76
Neva River, 26–28
Nikopol bridgehead, 29–30, 34
Normandy landings, 35, 46, 109, 114–115
Norwegian forces also Resistance, 54, 57

Oder River, 38, 94
Operations: Achse (Axe), 60, 84, 97, 112; Alphabet, 31; Bagration, 32, 35–36, 40, 47, 50, 91; Bettina, 114; Birke (Birch), 47, 50; Cheerful, 119; Crusader, 9–10; Edelweiss, 17; Eilbote I (Urgent Message I), 15; Eilbote II (Urgent Message II), 15; Frühling (Spring), 114; Frühlingsanfang (Start of Spring), 75; Frühlingssturm (Spring Storm), 107; Frühlingswind (Spring Wind), 13; Harling, 95; Husky, 60, 95; Korporal, 113; Kuckucksei (Cuckoo's Egg), 15; Kugelblitz (Lightning Ball), 86–87, 99; Maibaum (May Tree), 88–89; Margarethe, 31, 102; Mincemeat, 88, 95; Nachtigall (Nightingale), 115; Nordlicht (Northern Lights) (Finland), 47, 50; Nordlicht (Northern Lights) (Leningrad), 25–26; Nordwind (North Wind), 119, 121; Ochsenkopf (Oxhead), 16; Ratweek, 91; Rösselsprung (Little Horse Jump), 89; Rübezahl, 88, 90; Saturn, 27; Save, 88; Schneesturm (Snowstorm), 87; Schwarz (Black), 79, 81–82, 89, 96; Sinyavino, 26; Tanne (Fir Tree), 47fn; Tauziehen (Tug of War), 119; Torch, 13–14; Uranus, 27; Wacht am Rhein (Rhine Watch),119; Waldläufer (Forest Runner), 74; Waldrausch (Noises of the Forest), 87; Wegweiser (Signpost), 88; Wehrwolf, 107; Winterende (End of Winter), 75; Zitadelle (Citadel), 29
Orel, 32–33
Ostwall (East Wall), 29–30

Pemsel, Gen Max-Josef, 50
Petersen, Dr Wilhelm, 43, 84
Pflaum, Gen Karl, 113, 117
Phleps, Gen Artur, 76, 79–80, 82, 86, 89, 92, 97
Po Valley, 67–70, 75
Poglavnik Pavelic (Ante Pavelić), 109
Polish forces, 63, 72
    II Corps, 63; Resistance, 72
Poljana, battle of, 108
Prague, 121fn
Pripyat Marshes, 35; River, 34–35

Rapido River, 61–62
Red Air Force, 37–38
Red Army, 17, 20, 27, 29, 32, 35, 37–38, 40–41, 55–56, 77, 90, 92, 94, 103
    1st Ukrainian Front, 37; 2nd Shock Army, 27; 4th Ukrainian Front, 37; 5th Shock Army, 29; 8th Army, 27; 14th Army, 55; 38th Army, 37; 57th Army, 92; 67th Army, 27; partisans, 19, 38, 44
Red Orchestra, 25
Rendulic, Gen Lothar, 47, 50, 57–58, 84
Rhine River, 119–121
Rhône River, 115–116
Ringel, Gen Julius "Papa", 60–61, 63, 69, 106

Rokossovsky, Mar Konstantin, 37
Romanian Army, 17, 19, 24–24, 29, 31, 40–41
    2nd ID, 19, 27; 2nd MD, 17, 29
Rome, 8, 64–65
Rommel, Gen Erwin, 12–13
Rostov-on-Don, 17
Rzhev, (Rschew) also Pocket, 28, 32

Saarland, 120
Salerno landing, 60
Sarajevo, 81–82, 84, 86–90, 105, 107–108, 110
Sauberzweig, Gen Karl-Gustav, 85–86, 89, 94, 102, 109, 112
Schlemmer, Gen Hans, 116
Schörner, Gen Ferdinand, 30, 35, 38, 45
Schrank, Gen August Max-Günther, 63, 116
Sevastopol, 29
Sinyavino (Heights), 26–27
Skorzeny, Otto, 89
Slovak forces also partisans, 37, 41
Stalin, Joseph, 60, 95
Stalingrad also battle of, 13, 22–23, 27–28
Suez Canal, 8–9, 11
Syrmian Front, 105, 107

Tatra Mountains, 41
Taygetos Mountains, 99
Thessalonica, 80, 99
Tito, Josip Broz, 75, 77–78, 80–82, 84–94, 104, 106, 108, 110
Titovka River, 45, 55
Tobruk, 11
Todt Organization, 58, 68
Trieste, 11, 70–71, 75
Troppau (Fortress), 39, 41
Tunis, 14–116

US Army, 13–16, 35, 41, 59–64, 67–70, 73, 88, 90, 115, 118–121, 123
    Seventh Army, 119; VI Corps, 121; 1st AD, 73; 3rd ID, 119; 10th MD, 88; 34th ID, 16; 36th ID, 63; 45th Thunderbird ID, 120; 70th ID, 120; 85th ID, 69; 88th ID, 88; 94th ID, 121; 179th ID, 120

Vercors plateau, 69, 111–116
Vistula River, 36, 41
Vitebsk, 28, 33
Volkhov Front, 7, 26–27
Volksdeutsche, 74, 120
von Hengl, Gen Ritter, 45
von Hößlin, Gen Hans Wilhelm, 75
von Kluge, FM Günther, 32
von Le Suire, Gen Karl Hans, 22fn–24, 41
von Manstein, FM Erich, 25, 29
von Pannwitz, Gen Helmuth, 105
von Stettner Ritter von Grabenhofen, Gen Walter, 20, 22–23, 96–99, 104
von Weichs, FM Maximilian, 84
Vosges Mountains, 117–118, 120–121

Warsaw uprising, 36, 72
Weber, Gen Friedrich, 14–16
Wehrmacht
    Army Group: A, 17, 22, 26; Center, 26, 32, 34–35, 40–41, 50, 90; E, 80, 92–94, 103, 105, 108; F, 84; G, 115–116; Heinrici, 38; Ligurien, 65, 116–117; North, 25–27, 31, 51, 60; North Ukraine, 28, 31, 35–36, 40; Oberrhein, 119; South, 17, 27–29, 31–32, 107, 116; South Ukraine, 28, 31, 40, 91
    Armee: 1.PzA, 27, 29; 2., 34–35; 2.PzA, 84, 89, 107; 4., 33; 5.PzA, 14–15; 6., 27, 29, 40, 90, 106–107; 8., 73, 87; 9., 94; 10., 68; 11., 26; 12. 79–80; 14., 68; 17., 17, 38; 18., 26–28; 19., 115, 119; 20.Geb.A, 46–47, 50, 54, 57–59; 21. (Armee Norwegen), 58; Panzerarmee Afrika (*also* DAK), 9–14, 16, 95
    Armeekorps: AOK 14, 68; AOK Norwegen, 42, 44, 49; IV.AK, 27, 29; IV.PzK, 90; XVII.AK, 29, 31; XVIII. AK, 55; XI.AK, 17, 94; XV. Kosaken-Kavallerie-Korps, 105; XIX.PzK, 69; XXII.AK, 106; XXIII.AK, 34; XXIV. AK, 107; XXIX.AK, 31–31; XXX.AK, 26–27; XXXIV. AK, 108; XXXVI.AK, 45, 55;

XXXX.PzK, 39; XXXXII.AK, 36; XXXXIV.AK, 17–18, 20, 23, 28; XXXXVIII.AK, 36, 38; LII.AK, 31; LVI.PzK, 35; LVII.PzK, 17; LXIV.AK, 113; LXV.AK (Militärbefehlshaber Serbien),.79; LXVIII.AK, 94, 106; LXIX.Res.AK, 84; LXXVI.PzK, 67–69; LXXV. AK, 116; LXXXII.AK, 121; LXXXXVII.AK (OZAK), 70, 74–75; XC.AK, 120; XCI. AK, 107–108; Müller, 92; Orientkorps, 8–9, 11, 84, 107
Gebirgskorps: II.Geb.-AK, 64; IX. Waffen-Geb.-AK der SS (Kroatisches), 89, 92; XV.Geb.-AK, 79, 84, 86–87; XVIII.Geb.-AK, 47, 52; XIX. Geb.-AK, 49–50, 55; XXI. Geb.AK, 84, 103; XXII.Geb.- AK, 95, 98, 102; XXXVI. Geb.-AK, 49; XXXXIV.Geb.- AK, 28; XXXXIX.Geb.-AK, 17, 23–24, 28–29, 37–38, 41; LI.Geb.-AK, 64, 69, 118; V.SS-Gebirgs-Armee-Korps, 86–87, 89–90, 94
Gebirgsdivision: 1. Volks-Geb-Div *see* I.GD; 1.GD, 17–24, 33, 61, 79, 81–83, 86–88, 90–94, 96–100, 104, 106–108, 120; 2.GD, 33, 45, 49, 51, 55–56, 59, 119–121; 3.GD, 26–27, 29–31, 34, 37, 40–41, 49; 4.GD, 17, 19–24, 28–29, 37–38, 40–41; 5.GD, 26–27, 60, 62–64, 66–67, 69m 113–118; 6.GD, 45, 50, 55–56, 59; 6.SS-GD "Nord," 42–45, 47, 50, 52–56, 59, 92, 106fn, 117, 118, 120–122; 7.GD, 33, 45–47, 50, 52, 57, 59; 7. SS-Geb.-Frw.-Div Prinz Eugen, 76–79, 80–84, 86–94, 97, 103–105, 107–108; 8.GD, 65–66, 69–70, 75, 115, 117; 9.GD (Ost), 106–108; 13.(mus.) Waffen-Division Handschar, 73 85–86, 88–97, 106fn, 108–109, 112; 13. SS-Geb.-Frw.-Div, 87–88; 21. SS-Geb-Div Skanderbeg, 88, 90, 102–103, 105, 107–108; 23. Waffen-Geb-Div der SS (Kroatische Nr. 2) Kama, 89,

91–93; 24. Waffen-Geb-Div der SS, 71, 74–75; 157.Res.- Div, 69, 74, 111–117; 188. GD, 75
Jägerdivisionen: 1.SJD, 35–39; 28.JgD, 31; 97.JgD, 18, 23, 25, 28, 30–31, 34, 36–39; 101. JgD, 28; 104.JgD, 98; 114.JgD, 64, 120; 117.JgD, 106; 118. JgD, 81–82, 84; Brandenburg, 9, 23, 65, 81, 86–87, 89–90, 96, 99, 102, 104, 109; Fallschirmjäger, 61, 63, 89; Sonderverband (SdVbd) 288, 8–14; Sonderverband Bergmann, 36, 108
Kriegsmarine, 103, 105, 109
Luftwaffe, 11, 17, 33, 38, 42, 59, 75, 77, 81–82, 98–99, 103, 106–107, 109
    IV. Fliegerkorps, 17; 11. Luftwaffen-Felddivision, 99; 91.(Luftlande) ID, 109
OKW, 88, 85
OZAK *see* LXXXXVII.AK
Polizei (Ordnungspolizei), 42, 53–55, 70–72, 74, 77, 96, 99, 101, 113, 118
SD (Sicherheitdienst), 112, 114, 117
Waffen-SS, 45, 53–54, 56, 59, 72, 75–77, 79, 89–90, 94, 96, 102–103, 106, 108, 110, 120
Winter War (Russo-Finnish War), 32
Wittmann, Gen August, 29, 104, 106

Yugoslav forces, 75–78, 80–95, 104, 106–108, 110
    Yugoslav National Army (JNA) *also* Yugoslav Army of Liberation, 77–78, 104
        III Proletarian Corps, 88; 16th Communist D, 88; 17th Communist D, 88
    partisans (Titoists), 76, 78, 82–95, 106–108, 110
    Chetniks, 78, 80–82, 87–90, 92, 106

Zagreb, 87, 93–94, 108
Zhukov, Mar Georgi, 27